Bringing together voices from across Turtle Island, a groundbreaking collection of letters from Indigenous writers, activists, and thinkers—to their ancestors, to future generations, and to themselves.

———————————

Drawing on the wisdom and personal experience of its esteemed contributors, this first-of-its-kind anthology tackles complex questions of our times to provide a rich tapestry of Indigenous life, past, present, and future. The letters explore the histories that have brought us to this moment, the challenges and crises faced by present-day communities, and the visions that will lead us to a new architecture for thinking about Indigeneity. Taking its structure from the medicine bundle— tobacco, sage, cedar, and sweetgrass—it will stir and empower readers, as well as enrich an essential and ongoing conversation about what reconciliation looks like and what it means to be Indigenous today.

A
Steady
Brightness
of
Being

A Steady Brightness of Being

Truths, Wisdom,
and Love from
Celebrated
Indigenous Voices

EDITED BY
SARA SINCLAIR &
STEPHANIE SINCLAIR

PENGUIN

an imprint of Penguin Canada, a division of Penguin Random House Canada Limited

Canada • USA • UK • Ireland • Australia • New Zealand • India • South Africa • China

First published 2025

Penguin Canada
A division of Penguin Random House Canada
320 Front Street West, Suite 1400
Toronto, Ontario, M5V 3B6, Canada
penguinrandomhouse.ca

The authorized representative in the EU for product safety and compliance is Penguin Random House Ireland, Morrison Chambers, 32 Nassau Street, Dublin D02 YH68, Ireland, https://eu-contact.penguin.ie

LIBRARY AND ARCHIVES CANADA CATALOGUING IN PUBLICATION

Title: A steady brightness of being : truths, wisdom, and love from celebrated Indigenous voices / Sara Sinclair and Stephanie Sinclair, editors.
Names: Sinclair, Sara, editor | Sinclair, Stephanie (Stephanie L.), editor.
Identifiers: Canadiana (print) 20250153920 | Canadiana (ebook) 20250157659 |
    ISBN 9780735250369 (hardcover) | ISBN 9780735250376 (EPUB)
Subjects: LCSH: Indigenous peoples—Canada. | LCSH: Indigenous peoples—Canada—
    Ethnic identity. | LCSH: Indigenous peoples—Canada—Social conditions. |
    CSH: Indigenous letters (English)—21st century.
Classification: LCC E78.C2 S74 2025 | DDC 305.897/071—dc23

Cover and interior design by Kate Sinclair
Typeset in Portrait by Sean Tai
Cover images: Alanah Jewell, Morningstar Designs

Printed in Canada

10 9 8 7 6 5 4 3 2

Penguin
Random House
PENGUIN CANADA

For everyone trying to find their way home, trying to connect the past and present, and trying to heal, preserve, and celebrate who we are.

Contents

A
Steady
Brightness
of
Being

Introduction

It's October of 2024, and I'm in Victoria, British Columbia. I'm sitting by the water and thinking of my grandfather, Elmer Sinclair, a survivor of Fort Alexander Residential School. This morning, I went to where he and my grandmother rest. It's something I have been longing to do, and something I have avoided for some time. I have learned so much in the almost decade since he passed, and I wanted to express what I wish I had had the chance to say when he was alive, hoping his spirit might receive it. As I left the cemetery, I got a text from my cousin Niigaan Sinclair, sharing that Murray Sinclair's health had taken a dangerous turn and I should be preparing myself.

Now, I'm sitting by the water thinking about what I didn't say to my grandfather, and what I haven't said to Murray. I don't know that I will have the chance to express it all, but I know that there is still so much I want to say. So, I want to do what many people do when there are things left unsaid, or when we don't know how to say those things, or when the people we need aren't within reach: I want to write a letter.

A few years ago my sister and co-editor, Sara Sinclair, published a book called *How We Go Home: Voices from Indigenous North America*. In her work to publicize the book, she did a TEDx Talk and opened her speech by comparing how intergenerational trauma has been handled on both sides of our family. On our maternal side, our grandmother, who we called Bubby, was a Holocaust survivor who did years of work on her own trauma and shared her story with us openly. For comparison, Sara then looked at our paternal grandfather, who, as a residential school survivor, carried lifelong shame not just about his trauma but about his identity. He kept it all in, leaving only a silence in the shape of questions. It is stories that give shape to a life. But because he never talked about it, my father didn't inherit stories; he inherited shame.

As we grew up, it became explicitly clear that Bubby seemed to heal through telling her story and that so many stories untold by Indian residential school survivors meant so much history unhealed and unknown, including within our family.

The impact of this led to both of us, and our younger sister Minoway, growing interested in connecting the past to the present; in our professional lives, Sara and I work to amplify stories like our grandfather's. We know from our own family's experience that when traumatic events occur in cultures and are left undiscussed, it's not just the stories about the traumas that don't get passed down. The transfer of other cultural knowledge is disrupted, too. Our grandfather, for decades, didn't share stories about his own family or his young life, because he was taught to be ashamed of being an "Indian."

Part of the learning, begun by our father and continued by us, is to more deeply understand that many Indigenous people alive today have grown up at some distance from their ancestors' stories. This is a direct and intentional consequence of colonization, of which the Indian residential schools were an important weapon. For many, being Indigenous is a journey toward reclamation and continuance of language, knowledge, and nationhood.

We want to play a part in preserving and amplifying our stories and celebrating our relations. We want to understand all this history, to know both its burden and beauty. This book is an offering along this journey. Structured as a medicine bundle, with each letter representing a traditional medicine—tobacco, cedar, sweetgrass, or sage—this anthology is an entry point to connections. We hope these words might also move you toward conversations about Indigenous history, strength, and life, conversations many of us struggle to begin. The contributors in this book have written letters that cross great distances, whether geographic or metaphysical. Some have written to ancestors, relatives they've lost, or relatives they never met. Some have written to generations yet unborn and some to the land. They all say something the letter writer longs to express, that wouldn't work in any other form. The letters are an invitation to join the authors in this intimate space. I hope you'll meet us there.

Dear Murray, Mazina Giizhik-iban (the One Who Speaks of Pictures in the Sky),

I'm writing to you from Victoria. I'm sitting in a mostly empty hotel restaurant looking out at the water. It's my first time here in this city, and I wish I knew where my grandparents had lived. I wish I knew so much more than I do about their lives. I wish it had felt okay to ask questions.

I'm here in part to promote your book in Vancouver next week. You are struggling in the hospital, and I've just been told by Niigaan that things have taken a bad turn. I don't know what that means, but I'm sitting here waiting, hoping you aren't in pain, in some ways hoping you let go. You have fought enough; you have fought so tirelessly for all of us.

This morning, I went to see where my grandparents rest. They are in a beautiful garden surrounded by fountains and enormous, gorgeous Douglas fir trees. There is peace there. I sat in the rain and thought about my grandfather Elmer and your father, Henry—the brothers, what they endured at Fort Alexander, how they both left the school poisoned by shame and self-loathing and deep, deep trauma. I never knew Henry, but Elmer always seemed so big and powerful. My dad always retreated to a place I didn't know how to reach when Elmer came to visit, and I resented that. I remember being told why my dad feared his father, but I wasn't told what had happened, why Elmer was wounded in the first place, or how that wound had turned into rage. I had no compassionate understanding of our family history.

I wanted to go see Elmer today to say that I am sorry. I am sorry for not asking him questions about his life before the school. I am sorry for not helping him to remember what the school stole from him. I am sorry for not trusting him, for holding him at a distance when he needed open arms and love so desperately. I am sorry for resenting him, for not holding space for him to listen to his stories, to his testimony.

The last time I saw Elmer was when my grandmother died. They were married for sixty-nine years; she died weeks before their seventieth anniversary. He wept and wept, sitting alone. I walked to him, took his hand in mine, and sat with him while he cried.

That night, the family all went out for some food, and one of my father's brothers got drunk, angry, and threatening. He was fixated on my father and looked like a wild cat ready to pounce. Another moment when our family should have been there for Elmer, destroyed by alcoholism, rage, and shame. We all let him down again that day. It was only a few months later that Elmer died alone in a hospital room. I didn't fly back.

The first time you came to Toronto for media around the Truth and Reconciliation Commission, I listened to your conversation with Connie Walker, and something in me awakened. I then read and read and read, and suddenly parts of my life began to make sense in ways they never had before; parts of my father's life made sense, and parts of Elmer's life made sense. You looked so wounded, so different from when I had seen you last. Over those years, you gave this country your health, your spirit. Did this country deserve you?

I know you would want me to say yes and that we must continue to do the work and walk the path, but today, when I think of you in that hospital room in Winnipeg, I am angry. You are only seventy-three. You have struggled for so many years to manage a body with so much weight of responsibility that it became too hard to carry. And I know that your losing Katherine might mean losing you; you may not want to live without her, just like Elmer after his wife died.

But before you go, I want you to know that over the last few years, as we worked on your book, I felt like I finally got to listen to our family's stories and history with openness, pride, and a true understanding of why and how things turned out the way they did. I have become a better person for having spent this time with you. I am so grateful. Your wisdom, generosity, and raw empathy have shaped our country immeasurably. And I'm so sorry that your service has come at the cost of your health, of your life. I'm so sorry for all you had to endure yourself, for the trauma you had to carry for so many others. Please know that we are a better country because of you. And we are all grateful to you for giving our community a voice and the energy to fight for survival. We are still here.

Before you go, I want to tell you that I love you. I'm proud to be a Sinclair. When I saw you a few weeks ago, I showed you a video of my daughter, and you said, "Wow, that's a Sinclair face." My children can celebrate their Indigeneity; they are safe, they can learn about their history and culture, because of you.

Before you go, I promise to honour your legacy, to continue the work, knowing it will take generations. But I will do what I can.

Before you go, let me say thank you, and let me promise to be tireless, to be brave, to work for change with grace, to be kind, to be good, to rise above the clouds and think of you every time I look to the sky.

Stephanie

Tobacco

TERESE MARIE MAILHOT   *To Indians Now and*
                                       Forever Surviving

We come from an innumerable landscape of light and dark. The majority of our composition—oxygen, carbon, hydrogen, nitrogen, calcium,
phosphorus, potassium, sulphur, sodium, chlorine, and magnesium—
derives from stars and supernovas. I like to think about the stories of
Star Children. Sometimes my baby asks me about the spirit and how
it's formed, which is a deep consideration. I have no answers, only
questions, fantasies, and ideas given to me by women who left room
for debate. The women who raised me were residential school survivors and rebels and scholars and Christians—a group of women who
would not take shit, not for long, anyway. We are women who run
away, leave, fight back, talk back, act back, and it's all for the future
of our being.

Time is a continuum, and we are on it, baby. Our living and dying is
real, no matter the erasure, no matter how an anthropologist might
delight in our bones, and dumb down our art, our living, or our hearts.

As I sit now, on this porch, my baby (he's nine) is making chimichurri with his uncle in the kitchen. I feel the wind outside and hear their laughter.

I often look at my children and wonder what words I need to leave behind to spare them pain and ponderance. I often remember my mother and her teachings—the things she said when we picked sage, the protocols and philosophic ideas she'd sprout at random that now don't feel so random, as I raise my own babies and teach them to honour the Land.

What a life we've made as Indians and as survivors whose grandmothers were called heathens. Whose grandmothers were forsaken. Whose grandmothers sometimes felt radically lost and abandoned.

My grandmother was carried to residential school by a nine-year-old cousin who made a promise to look out for her. To think of the pain feels absolute—I think of the way her cousin adopted her as his own daughter, and the way my mom called him "Grampa Crow," and how he told me old stories, and he treated me like I mattered. His love carried over to me and my brother, and it lives in my sons now.

How beautiful to see our continuance through this lively lens. I feel our nature and star being, watching my kids move like lightning around me, and they fall soft like stars during their come-down hours, beneath the moonlight in their safe beds.

For so long we have fought to exist, and for what? For everything. For every dance around the sun. Each year we get, we do rejoice.

I believe we are a steady brightness of being, like a running wheel of light. Native people carry power. All Indigenous people are bound to something inextricably connected to the land, the sky, and the universe itself. All our teachings will tell you we are one with the stars. That we come from that light. Some nations could pinpoint the galaxies from which we derive. Some people were so exact about our relationship to the universal state of being—we are so transcendent and beautiful, and destined to be. I believe in us. I believe in the seventh generation—the White Buffalo Calf Woman—in Sas'qets, and in every story of our creation and the time before time. I believe so wholeheartedly that sometimes I keep my beliefs secret from white people, academics, scholars, therapists, or anyone who might use this belief and knowledge to lock me up. Isn't it strange that our beliefs are still forbidden in some way? Do you feel the weight of colonization? Or have you come to break those ties down and build up from there? I love us, and I believe we are divine—existing by chance, born from some giant red ancient star, set to earth: a fire with mission, catapulting light to form what compels us to keep going. No matter what, we keep going. I keep wondering, as my son keeps asking me, where we go when we die. I don't know. The contemplation, too, keeps me going. Each day I try to derive meaning from this life and give that life to my babies. We have to keep going, right?

At age seven my son memorized the periodic table. He used to assign people elements, and that's how I knew his brilliance was complex and poetic and Indian. He called me Cn: something heavy and combustible, and radioactive, too—dangerous, but necessary. My mother used to teach me how all people are elemental, and I didn't get it at first. Now, much older, prone to loneliness, long trudges, and waterfalls, I get why

I was named Little Mountain Woman—the name tells me about myself so well. The mountain is where I go when I need power, healing, and restitution, and my life has felt mostly uphill. My hope is that there will be a wonderful, spry trek downhill someday, of mostly soft valley and beauty. I can't say.

My hope is that we continue, that life gets easier, that we never stop fighting for our continuum, our ways of being, and that we never forget where we come from, because we are so elemental and good. My hope is that our stories, our names, and star nature all continue on and on, and on and on—forever.

T

Someone told me a story once and it changed me forever. I don't think it was meant be that kind of story, but something in the way she told it created such a visceral experience for me that I often remember it as the moment I started seeing things differently.

Many years ago, when I was a professional dancer, I was rehearsing at a studio in downtown Toronto. I was working with an Anishinaabe choreographer and a few other Indigenous dancers. We had all been developing this piece for some time, so we were very comfortable with one another. We had created a safe space to talk and listen, to laugh and cry, so we all shared freely. It was a special group of women.

The choreography was demanding and the subject matter was triggering. We would often get into deep conversations about family trauma and intergenerational grief, ceremony and art, healing and recovery. The days were long and our bodies and hearts were sore, but we believed in the process and we felt so empowered by the work.

One lunch break, we all walked down the street to a hole-in-the-wall shawarma joint that only offered takeout. The place was so small that the five of us had to squeeze in and huddle together while we ordered our food. It was there, in the most unassuming of places, that this life-changing story was told, while Middle Eastern music played in the background and the smell of falafels filled the air.

The story came out of a conversation about how we connect with those who came before us and how they connect with us. One of the women started talking about this time when her family went out onto the land for a three-day fasting ceremony. It was a hard one. She said it was one of the hardest. She could hear the wailing and crying from different families around her. So many people releasing, processing, and purging. On the final day, she entered the sweat lodge. She prayed and talked to her ancestors, calling upon all of them.

As we waited for our food orders to come up, still listening intently, she spoke about the darkness of the lodge. I was transported into that world, far from the fluorescent lights and loud music of downtown Toronto. I could see the glowing rocks; I could smell the burning medicines. It reminded me of the magic and awe I have felt in the lodge and how that ceremony has the power to transmute suffering into energy to live and thrive. I thought that was the fullest part of the experience, the most I could hope for in that space. Until she told us what happened next. She made it through three rounds of songs and prayers and stayed inside the lodge through the break, even when they opened the door. When the fourth round began, she prayed harder and called on her ancestors even more. At the end of the round, the door flap opened and the light poured in. But instead of seeing trees or the firepit or the earth outside the lodge, she saw faces and more faces—lines of people that travelled so far back she couldn't see the end of the line. The door to the East—the place where we leave the spirit world to travel to the physical world when we are born, the place where each day begins—was crowded, packed, overflowing with ancestors upon ancestors looking in at her. My breath caught in my throat. Tears filled my eyes. My skin tingled and my heart throbbed. This is what knowing feels like. It was as if her story proved something that I needed to know was real. No matter how much I believed or prayed, no matter how many spirit stories I'd heard before, no matter how much I spoke to them over the years, every once in a while, I wondered if they really were there. In my loneliest times and in my darkest times, I would call upon them and believed they were; but in all honesty, sometimes I wasn't sure.

For some reason, that impersonal and unsentimental setting was the perfect place for my most spiritual teaching: they are there, they are always there—the army of ancestors. I remember when she said, "All these faces that just kept going," and I knew exactly who they were. From that day on, I never doubted again.

I return to that image of ancestors in the doorway often. I continue to tell this story with the hope that it might unlock the same knowing in someone else. The reminder that we are forever connected and protected by those who came before us. It changed the way I walked in the world, the risks I took and the dreams I dared to dream. I stand taller, speak louder, and dance harder because I know they are there. My army of ancestors.

It doesn't mean bad things won't happen or that hardships will get easier, but it does mean that I have the power to rise to all of it. Every moment of glory and every moment of pain, I can feel them around me, and it makes everything possible. There is an entire spiritual force organized with one specific purpose—to keep me moving forward.

And so I do.

BILLY-RAY BELCOURT

Dear Boreal Forest (specifically,
the stretch of it in northwest
Alberta I grew up on)

According to scientists, you appear to be shrinking, retreating north-ward in response to a warming planet. First, I am sorry, though an apology only does so much when the instigators of climate disaster carry on unabatedly.

When I first read about this phenomenon, my heart broke. I thought about the ways Cree people—specifically, the Crees of northern Alberta—are a forest people; we are bound up in you, we co-determine one another, though you know this already.

When I was a kid, you were a whole world I had access to. You were my world. I hid inside the forest and waited for the future. I was of you, a part of you, but we're taught not to believe this with any seriousness. I forgot this fact of my personhood for many years because being human means I am forgetful and flawed.

I had to become a poet before I realized the forest had made me a poet already. When I first really took sight of the trembling poplars—the way their leaves tremble even when the day is completely still—something in me shifted; it was like being filled with light, with pure knowledge.

In the winter, when all your leaves have fallen, there is a beauty in your exposure I want to learn from. It has often reminded me of the possibility of survival, which is innate and difficult to destroy—despite how often people and corporations will endeavour to do so. You are intimate with cycles of loss and rebirth; this is as inevitable as air, as the blueness of the sky. We cannot take this aspect of your being, your sentience, for granted. This is a quality of living we must defend and maintain reverence for.

When I describe you, I seem to always fall short of grasping something abstract, something non-material. Maybe things are better that way. Maybe we do not need to understand or articulate everything.

Like the lake around which you live, you precede me, you precede Cree people, but you will also outlast us. You are both our past and future, our living and future ancestors. I appreciate the clarity of the term "future ancestor" because it means that I will one day be magnificent, like you.

To think of you is also to think of my kokum, who has lived alongside you her whole life (as have most of my kin). For the last few summers, when I have visited her and other family members in northern Alberta, the skies have often been filled with smoke. It has felt catastrophic, apocalyptic. It has hurt to breathe. We have had to learn how to breathe differently, as I know you have as well. To breathe differently together is our ongoing work.

We are all under siege, though not all of us can flee.

I once wrote a story about a Cree man who enters the forest as a way to grieve. After just a few minutes, he realizes that the forest also grieves and that he must bear some of that grief as well. I do not quite know how to do this myself. I suppose that I will spend the rest of my life trying to figure it out.

Yours,
Billy-Ray

Giizhemanito gizhawenimig.
The Creator loves you.

There is proof of this everywhere in your life. Learning to recognize these signs is one of the greatest gifts we can learn to accept.

Consider the galactic odds, so long they stretched themselves to the point of nearly breaking, the right elements interacting on a planet at the right distance from a star the right size just so life could be created on Earth. Consider how those odds were compounded that life would subsequently evolve over millions of generations to develop such amazing feats of complexity as the eyes which allow us to see, the thumbs which allow us to grip, and the minds which allow us to dream. Consider then how those odds would be further multiplied to see human beings come together over untold millennia to develop the traditions and ceremonies which deliver us to the moments of beauty that we walk through in our lives.

The Dakota Sundance and the movement of thousands of uniquely shaped tobacco ties and coloured flags as a breeze rustles the branches of the tree of life just before it is raised. You will look to the Elders deep in prayer as they offer the heart of the buffalo. You will look at the sandy consistency of the earth in this part of the world and know you are in that sacred place.

The Métis fiddle playing the Maytwayashing Waltz in all its bittersweet glory as you paddle your canoe across still waters under the light of a setting summer sun. You will be moved by the melody and rhythm and remark on how two traditions, and many more, have come together in these lands. You will know they are intertwined like the infinity symbol, and they belong here. And you will know this is good.

The Anishinaabe Jingle Dress delivering healing to the Nation under the bright lights of a Pow-wow's evening session. You will study the dozens of dancers in their regalia, each telling a story of the dancer's individual identity and cultural background through colour, pattern, and design. Their steps will tell you something of how they walk through life. Even the ways in which they tie and fix their hair will testify to the amazing diversity of creation. In this moment you will know what it is to have a vision—a gift from the Creator so powerful that thousands of people you never meet carry on your dream long after you are gone.

Your life is a sacred gift. It embodies a vision. Perhaps your own, perhaps one belonging to your ancestors, perhaps both.

Remember those who came before you and the sacrifices they made. Many times they were just trying to get by. Yet, seen from the Creator's eye, they must have also been pushing forward so that you could be here today with the chance to be who you are—exactly as you are.

Remember the Survivors who endured things we can scarcely imagine. Remember their humanity, remember their shortcomings, and remember the love they hold for you. They love you, just as you will love your descendants. I pray they show you this love while they are alive, and if their lives were too hard for them to do so, then I hope you will forgive them once they are gone.

Remember those who never came home.

This world is full of mountains to climb, oceans to swim in, and wonderful people to meet and make your life with. In these moments your heart will soar to its greatest heights, your body will feel to the limits of its senses, and your spirit will know its place in the universe.

Some of these moments will inspire you, some of these moments will hurt you, but either way, they ask you to keep going. It is in the spaces between these events and in the distances that span them that the signs of the gift you are to receive are revealed.

There will be heartache, such as the time you pour your heart into welcoming a little one into this world with a partner, only to be given a diagnosis of some health issue with this child. You will curse and pace and dwell on your feelings of stress. Your family will encourage you to listen to the medical advice and slow down. You will do so and the child will come home while you still carry that worry in your heart and in your mind.

You will get busy orienting your life around this little one. You will build a family, a career, and a meaningful path all with an eye toward ensuring this little person has what they need. At first this will mean the bare necessities of life such as food, water, clothing, and shelter. The child's emotional, cultural, and spiritual needs will also need nourishing. You will learn also to provide a model for how to carry themselves in life. You should teach them to hold their head high, to laugh heartily, and to be kind and generous.

You will get so busy carrying out these duties that decades will go by. Your family will grow, your career will progress, and you will notice how the years now pass a little more quickly. The love you feel for your children will be a love that you had never felt before, like a new colour or a new taste, but not just any new colour or taste—a most beautiful hue, a most delicious flavour. This love, unique among all loves, will propel you to do things you could barely imagine before you were a parent.

You will work, you will Sundance, you will coach. You will wake up early with your children, and you will rock them late into the night. As they grow up and encounter trials and tribulations of their own, you will take phone calls from worried friends or family and go for long drives on rainy nights to talk things over with your kids. You will tell your children how much you love them.

And then one day you will come home to find a letter you did not expect. You will open it and read the results of a medical test that tells you the health issue your child faced all those years ago is now in the past. Their body has grown strong and healthy, and they are thriving. You will sit at your kitchen table and shed tears alone. A burden that had been there for so long you had forgotten you were carrying it will have been lifted. You will say a prayer of thanks for the liberation you didn't know you needed. You will offer tobacco as you have been taught. Soon after, and without fanfare, you will continue on with the journey you have been walking those many years. Perhaps your path will be different, but I suspect some of the steps will be the same.

It is in these moments the Creator shows us.

Gizhaweminigoo.
You are loved.

—WK

Want to hear three deadly ancestor stories?

I grew up in Fort Smith, NWT, always hearing a story about my grand-father, Pierre Washie. I was told that he was adopted into the Tłįchǫ Nation after he became an orphan. The story goes that when he was a young man, he lost his entire family in the TB and influenza epidemics. Because he was on his own with his dog, he decided to travel with a wish to live among the Dogribs. (This is what we used to be called; we now call ourselves and are known as Tłįchǫ.) To get to Tłįchǫ territory, he and his dog had to travel through the mountains. This took many days. When he arrived to Tłįchǫ territory, he was met by a Tłįchǫ man who would not let him near the people, out of fear that my grandfather could be sick with TB and influenza (also known as the "mal du Fort Rae") and bring sickness to the people.

The Tłįchǫ man asked, through sign language, where my grandfather had come from. My grandfather explained that he'd travelled through the mountains with his dog and it had taken him a number of days to get to where he was standing. This surprised the man protecting the Tłı̨chǫ. To his knowledge, it took longer to travel through the mountains to get to the caribou hunting grounds, somewhere between the barrenlands and where the Dogrib lived, but it seemed that my grandfather had found a shortcut.

After a few days of observing my grandfather and making sure he was not sick, the man who guarded him was assigned by the head man of the Tłı̨chǫ to go back through the mountains and to find my grandfather's shortcut to the barrenlands. To everyone's delight, the shortcut worked. This shaved off precious time for the Tłı̨chǫ to travel back and forth to the caribou hunting grounds, and my grandfather was adopted into the Tłı̨chǫ Nation. My grandfather's Indian name is Wedzeèbàa, for "Big Ears" or "One Who Listens."

I remember my grandfather well. I miss him. Wedzeèbàa was a chanter and spoke very little English. I spoke very little Tłı̨chǫ when he and my late grandmother, Melanie Washie, were still alive, but I have recordings of our visits where my mom and uncles would translate what my grandparents shared with us.

I wrote a comic with Cree artist Kyle Charles celebrating my grandfather and the time he cured a small boy. The boy was taken to Wedzeèbàa because the boy had a stutter. My grandfather prayed for the boy and pulled a hummingbird of fire out of the boy's mouth. Many people witnessed this. The boy never stuttered again and still, to this day, prays with gratitude to my grandfather's memory.

Author Kieran Moore wrote a chapter about my grandfather in his book *Burnt Snow: My Years Living and Working with the Dene of the Northwest Territories* (Hancock House, 2020), titled "The Joker: Dzèhkw'ii," in which Kieran was invited to witness my ehtse perform a ceremony. It's a harrowing account of just how powerful and swift my grandfather was.

It is said that my late grandfather was a Mountain Dene. My late grandmother, Melanie, was Tłįchǫ. Her maiden name was "Football." Because we are a matrilineal society, we trace our bloodlines through our mother. This is why I say I am Tłįchǫ Dene.

And to my complete joy, this was confirmed in Edmonton, Alberta, Treaty 6 Territory, in the fall of 2024 by Sahtúgot'įnę Elder Fibbie Tatti: "Yes," she said, upon hearing my story about my grandfather being a Mountain Dene. "My father is a Mountain Indian. We heard about your grandfather already from our people. Because there was . . . sometimes children were abandoned, and like families took them, different families took them and that, and especially people that had no children or very . . . no relatives."

And we are so lucky to have our family tree documented. Through my grandmother, Melanie Football, her parents were Joseph Koyin-Football and Catherine Yatlayi. Joseph's parents were Jude T'aetsia Dryneck and Catherine Edatchie. Catherine's parents were Guillaume Yatlayi and Emerantine Indjole Konttsi.

Looking at our family tree, Adam Fwachi Washie and Elise Tsadzin must have traditionally adopted Pierre. Adam Fwachi's parents were

Andre Witchow and Julienne Tsel'in. Elise's parents were Marc Tsadzin and Palagie Tsenachie. And we are fortunate to have family tree information going back to our ancestors, such as Emerantine Indjole Konttsi, born in 1852 in Behchokǫ̀ (formerly known as Fort Rae, NWT). Thank goodness for our ancestors and thank goodness for our family archivists. Ora-naja Wah-Shee shared this family history with me. Mahsi cho, Cousin. And it is my Tłįchǫ language teacher, Georgina Franki, who helped me with the correct spelling of my grandfather's name in Tłįchǫ.

Okay, so are you ready for an equally deadly story that's ever good?

Years ago, my mom, Rosa Wah-Shee, worked with a woman in the Government of the Northwest Territories in Yellowknife.

After they retired, my mom was gifted something special from her friend that became deeply precious to our family and may hold a clue about the Tłįchǫ and the Navajo bond as extended family.

My mom shared with us that her friend had been in Navajo territory on vacation and was shopping for gifts for her family when she felt like she was being called to the back of the store. To her surprise, she discovered a picture that she knew she needed to acquire so it could be gifted to my mom.

In this photo is an Elder. She looks strong, but it's her eyes that get me. They've seen so much for one lifetime—maybe too much. She has my grandmother's hands, and I love her dress. Like the photos I see of our Tłįchǫ ancestors, she, too, wears a black shawl.

The bottom of the photo reads "Old Washie: Navajo Medicine Woman (1886)."

What is my mom's and my late ehtsi and ehtse's last name? Wah-Shee. My grandparents spelled it "Washie" because it means "Mountain."

My grandfather showed the Tłįchǫ the shortcut to the hunting and calving grounds of the caribou—the ekwo people—through the mountains.

We have the same last family name.

Why is this so important?

I had heard a story growing up that a long time ago the Dogrib had lost many of its people in a blizzard, and it was thought that they had discovered or were swept into a portal—a "Window Rock."

I was told about a theory that the Navajo have a "Window Rock" in the United States and that they, too, have a story about losing members of their people in a sandstorm or a portal through their Window Rock, and this is why our numbers one through ten are the same, why so many of our words are so similar—because we adopted one another when we magically showed up (like my grandfather and his dog).

Enter Sahtúgot'ı̨nę Elder Fibbie Tatti again. When I shared this story and the photo with Fibbie in Edmonton, she said she believed in the portals completely, and she also shared something with me that I have permission to share with you: "And I really believe that there is a portal. Like, there is, it's not just the white man's version. Like, they say that sometimes in the stars or on the land or stuff like that, you can go from here to there. You know why I believe that? Because the Elders say that that's what the caribou do. The caribou fold the land so they can go from here to there like that. So we look at the caribou and we think so, like, eh, okay. Like, they keep their feet really well, eh, the caribou, because they have long distances to walk. And we feel sorry for them, but we're not supposed to because they give themselves to us willingly. But they fold the land. So that's another way of a portal. But I also believe that you can go from here to there through the universe. I believe that."

Mahsi cho, Fibbie Tatti!! :) Holy canoley, am I ever grateful to you!!

When my mom's friend gifted her the portrait of Old Washie, she told her, "This is your ancestor. Pray to her. Share your sorrows, your worries, your dreams, your wishes. She'll listen." She told my mom to make copies of this photo for all of us in the family. Now when the chips are down or I start to feel lost, I pray to her and I speak to her. I share my worries, my anxiety, my hopes, and my dreams, and I do feel like she listens. Mahsi cho, Aunty. :)

And I wanted to share all of this with you. Sometimes, when we are asked about our ancestors, it can be hard to picture them. I urge you to go to the archivists in your family or online. Or why not travel to your heartlands and find what stories and medicines you need for peace and pride? Why not gather what you can and share it with your family, so that they can have someone or something to celebrate and cherish?

Share your worries and your dreams and goals with your ancestors. Think of what they saw in their lifetime and think of all that you are seeing in yours. We are not meant to travel this path alone, and I don't think our dearly departed or our ancestors are ever too far away for them to lean in and listen to you when you feel lost.

Sometimes late at night when I go stand out in our yard to look at the moon and stars, I think of the starlight that would bathe the mother of all Tłı̨chǫ holding her six puppies. I think of Old Washie, Navajo Medicine Woman in 1886, her silver hair glowing in moonlight as she made her way visiting. I think of that same star and moonlight bathing my grandfather and his dog as they made their way through their mountains to the Tłı̨chǫ, and I think of Adam Fwachi Washie and Elise Tsadzin, who traditionally adopted my grandfather, Pierre, and the first stars they walked under as a new family. I think of me holding your hand, Edzazii, our marvellous child and miracle, as we return home from a day in the ravine here in Edmonton, Alberta, Treaty 6 Territory, where we grow together as a family. These are your ancestors.

And this is my love letter to our ancestors—your ancestors.

Mahsi cho for reading this. I hope these stories inspire you to gather the medicines you need for your family, your community, and for future generations. We all have so very much to learn from one another.

With great respect to you, and to your family, and to the family of your heart,

Richard Van Camp
Tłįchǫ Dene
Proud son of Rosa Wah-Shee
Proud grandson of Pierre and Melanie Washie
Great-nephew to Old Washie, Navajo Medicine Woman (1886)

My friends lii nwaazh, it seems I've lived my whole life in relation to you, without ever giving you a word. I offer these now as a way of honouring your gifts, reminding myself of our connection. Though we haven't spoken, I have often tried to read your meaning as you traced out warnings or benedictions along the horizon—threatening storms, promising life-giving precipitation. I have tasted your rain-children on my outstretched tongue. I've discovered human faces within your folds, and animals and mountains and all kinds of miraculous things. I've stood in rivers and felt the cold vitality of moving water thrumming against my legs, without understanding that it was you, embracing me. Through you, and through the water within me, my body is an opening to sky.

I've been so ground-bound in my life, tied up in the struggles of the moment, weighed down by heavy history and a violent present and the prospect of erasure lurking always. The land is stolen; the land is there beneath our feet: that infuriating contradiction of colonial existence.

Land carved up, barricaded, reorganized, de-placed, advertised, bought, and sold—and yet still, we recognize it, and it recognizes us too. We water it with tears—what you might call our Children.

And sometimes in my anguish about the state of this land and the prospects for change, I look up to the sky and wonder what we can learn from you, who seem to disappear before our eyes, and yet you always come back. You are like the old stories in that way: seemingly ephemeral, but in fact incredibly strong, because you return, and return, and return. It makes me think we should all aspire to be cloudlike: transient eternal expressions of water, shapes always changing yet somehow connected to the infinite. Maybe that's what the Elders mean when they say Water is Life.

Once, my eyes watered as I stood at the edge of a bitumen mine, where the land had been stripped away for miles and the earth was cut open in enormous gashes. The air was thick with smoke and benzene and sulfur. Machines grumbled in the background, and electrical wires crackled above. There was no sign of life for as far as I could see, except the one thing that gave me hope, that reminded me I was human in that utterly inhuman place: a single cloud low on the horizon. It glowed with a strange radiance, so incongruous in that landscape of despair. I watched it for a long time as it made its way eastward, casting a slim shadow on the open earth, and I thought, "The clouds at least can never be colonized."

Of course, I was wrong. The reason for my error was right before me. The sky has been colonized already by billions of tonnes of carbon displaced from the land and funnelled into the air. You know this intimately, my relatives. Your territory has been invaded, your world changed by forces that come from far away, and you will continue to be affected for countless human generations. Some scientists even predict a future when clouds might be gone altogether, squeezed out of the atmosphere by CO_2. It's a world I struggle to imagine: without the water cycle, without a moderating influence on solar radiation, without the wondrous panoply of ever-changing beings overhead. And inevitably, without humans and so many of our kin.

I won't insult you with sorry. I am part of the damage, I know, even though I try to distance myself from it. But I will say this: the ones who forced us from our land, who installed the fences and drilled the wells and financed the mines—they thought we would disappear too. They banked on it. But we are still here. And I know we owe our survival to the relationships we've maintained with the land, despite all the forces that have tried to separate us from it. The land, and the sky. Which is to say, I believe in your return, always. I believe in the cycles, in the stories that make and move the world, and I know that you are part of them. As we are part of you.

—Warren Cariou

Sage

Dad died early Monday, November 4, 2024, at St. Boniface Hospital on Treaty 1 in Winnipeg, surrounded by all his family. He was seventy-three.

I miss him. I know you will, too. The Honourable Justice Murray Sinclair was a remarkable lawyer, judge, commissioner, and senator for you. He worked in your organizations, won so many of your awards, and travelled to communities where he visited, interacted with, and inspired and empowered many.

But to my sisters and me he was niibaabaa, Dad, and to his grandchildren he was mishom, Grandfather.

Regardless of how you knew him, though, he was a man who—from the second you met him—instantly made you feel special. He was someone you wanted to visit, spend time sharing food with, and listen to as he shared his many stories freely and with a generosity you never forgot.

He was an advocate, a fighter, a poet, an artist, and perhaps most of all: an educator. For most of his life he was the "first" in the rooms he walked into, which meant he spent a lot of time explaining, teaching, listening, and helping a country that didn't always want to hear what he had to say. This is a country that eventually began to crawl—and maybe even walk—due to his work as it listened, learned, and now takes up the many Calls to Action he inspired.

Dad didn't do this for personal gain though; he did this to embody the spirit of his traditional Anishinaabe name: Mazina Giizhik-iban, the One Who Speaks of Pictures in the Sky.

And speak of this he did.

He was born in 1951 on St. Peter's Indian Reserve near Selkirk, Manitoba. His parents were Henry (whose families came from Kihci-wâskâhikan, York Factory, and Nisichawayasihk Cree Nation, Nelson House) and Florence (whose family came from Manigotagan, Hollow Water First Nation).

After losing his mother at the age of one, he, along with his brothers, Richard and Henry Jr., and sister, Diane, were taken in by his grandparents, Henry James and Catherine Sinclair, who raised them. During these years, Murray's adventures with his brother Buddy and their dog Chum were legendary, especially when they would play tricks on their grandfather.

At the time, the children were watched over by the "big aunties": Bertha, Rose, Aurillia, Lorna, Louise, and Josephine, who was in charge of

Murray. Auntie Jo was a teacher who fostered in him a love of reading and education. Overall, though, it was Granny Cate who provided in Mazina Giizhik-iban a sense of family, generosity, and how to combine traditional teachings with institutions like the Catholic church.

As he grew up, Mazina Giizhik-iban experienced a great deal of racism but never lost his sense of hope, duty, and responsibility. These values led him to thrive in school (becoming valedictorian and graduating athlete of the year) and as a cadet (warrant officer first class).

He attended the University of Winnipeg before leaving his studies to care for Granny Cate and, eventually, his father, Henry. There, Mazina Giizhik-iban began working for the Selkirk Friendship Centre as a program organizer and bingo caller until being elected Interlake region vice-president of the Manitoba Métis Federation (MMF).

In 1973, Mazina Giizhik-iban was asked by then-Attorney General of Manitoba Howard Pawley to be his executive assistant. Showing interest in the law, he was encouraged to enter the University of Manitoba Faculty of Law in 1976. By his second year, he won the A.J. Christie Prize in Civil Litigation and was called to the Manitoba Bar in 1980, practicing civil and criminal litigation at his own law practice in Selkirk and firms in Winnipeg.

He also continued his work in politics, becoming the successful campaign manager of Elijah Harper—the first treaty Indian to be elected as an MLA, during the 1981 Manitoba election.

As a lawyer, Mazina Giizhik-iban specialized in representing Indigenous communities in land claims and criminal defences. As one of the first Indigenous lawyers in Canada, he would be mistaken by judges and prison officials as the accused instead of a lawyer.

As a result, Mazina Giizhik-iban began to speak out publicly about the mistreatment of Indigenous peoples in the justice system and worked with organizations like the Four Nations Confederacy, the Manitoba Human Rights Commission, the Assembly of Manitoba Chiefs, and the MMF. He also began to participate in contentious land rights negotiations and advocate in courts internationally. This also led to him being appointed to the Manitoba court in 1988 as Manitoba's first—and Canada's second—Indigenous judge.

After being appointed as a judge, Mazina Giizhik-iban worked with Justice Alvin Hamilton to create the Aboriginal Justice Inquiry (AJI), which examined Indigenous experiences with the justice system and examined the deaths of Helen Betty Osborne and J.J. Harper. The Inquiry's final report made 296 recommendations for changes within the justice system.

After returning to preside in courts across Manitoba—and in particular First Nations—Mazina Giizhik-iban was appointed to investigate the deaths of twelve children at Winnipeg's Health Sciences Centre during the Pediatric Cardiac Surgery Inquiry, finding that ten deaths were preventable.

Six years later Mazina Giizhik-iban was appointed to the province's Court of Queen's Bench—again, the first Indigenous judge given this honour.

In 2009, Mazina Giizhik-iban was appointed head commissioner of Canada's Truth and Reconciliation Commission alongside Dr. Marie Wilson and Chief Wilton Littlechild. The TRC investigated the accounts and impacts of Canada's residential school system and in 2015 offered 94 Calls to Action for widescale changes to all aspects of Canadian society.

Soon after the end of the TRC, Mazina Giizhik-iban was appointed to the Canadian Senate but continued his community work, performing an investigation into racism in the Thunder Bay Police. As a senator, Mazina Giizhik-iban successfully helped draft and pass legislation on water animal protection, LGBTQ2S+ rights, and Indigenous languages, rights, and child welfare jurisdiction.

In 2021, Mazina Giizhik-iban retired from the Senate and joined a law firm to mentor young Indigenous lawyers. He also became Chancellor of Queen's University and mediated negotiations for the multi-billion-dollar federal settlement compensating Indigenous children and families for being unfairly treated by Canada's child welfare systems.

Over his career Mazina Giizhik-iban received many honours, including nearly two dozen honorary degrees from universities, two National Aboriginal (now Indspire) Awards, a Symons Medal, the Peace Patron Award from the Mosaic Institute, the Mahatma Gandhi Prize for Peace, Canada's World Peace Award, and the Mandela Award, and he was appointed to the Order of Manitoba and the Order of Canada. Over decades he was instrumental in building organizations such as the John Howard Society, the Royal Canadian Cadets, Scouts Canada, the

Canadian Native Law Students Association, the Canadian Indian Lawyers Association (now the Indigenous Bar Association), the Social Planning Council of Winnipeg, the Ma Mawi Wi Chi Itata Centre, AbinochiZhawaynDakooziwin Ojibway Immersion Nursery School, the Selkirk Friendship Centre, the Manitoba Provincial Judges Association, the Manitoba Bar Association, the National Judicial Institute, the University of Manitoba Faculty of Law and the University of Winnipeg.

This, however, is just a short list of Dad's accomplishments—an impossibility for anyone to try and encapsulate in any way. I do, however, here in this letter, want to tell you a few things you don't know about him, his life, his work, and his loves. I want to tell you what he gave us—truly, what he gifted us, and left for us to do.

But first, I want to make a confession. It's a hard one and one that's taken me a long time to learn but came from the teachings of my dad's life and all of us who had a front-row seat to it.

It is this: I've been very angry at you, Canada.

I'm angry for the ways you took Dad from us.

I'm angry that he spent a lifetime dealing with this country's racism, division, violence, and genocidal actions.

I'm angry that he was the one working the hardest with leaders who treated fellow human beings so poorly and was often the sole voice of dignity against a wall of callousness. I'm angry that he didn't spend time doing what he loved to do—carpentry, by the way—and that he missed most of our lives as we gifted him to a country that didn't always treat him as a gift.

I confess this now not because I'm "over it" but in recognition that all Indigenous children of parents in that generation—and there are still so many of us today—have and are experiencing that same resentment. All of us have, in one way or another, sat at home while our parents and grandparents spent most of their lives fighting against institutions and laws to make sure we have safe places to live, clean water to drink, and languages to speak—when what we wanted more than anything was to have them at home, loving us.

It is only now that I, as a parent, can see why he did what he did. I see this humbly as I realize I am left to struggle as he did and continue the work of fighting for justice and truth. This is an ongoing responsibility for those of us left on this path, following in the many paths forged by our parents, grandparents, and indeed all of our ancestors. This is work he and I spoke about many times, especially during his last few months in the hospital.

One afternoon, in fact, I asked him why he did what he did, why he spent so much time on the road, going to events, giving speeches, going to the courts of the hundreds of AJI, Pediatric Inquest, or TRC gatherings, or working in the Senate. I asked him if it was a sense of duty like he learned in the Air Cadets, a sense of responsibility like he learned in the legal profession, or a sense of the "bigger picture" he got when he became a father.

He told me, simply: "I felt called."

He told me the story of Granny Cate sitting him down the day he told her he wasn't going to go into the priesthood. Refusing to sign a permission slip to let him enrol in university, she finally signed it after three days of him asking, but made him make a promise: that he would always work for the people.

"She looked me straight in the eyes," he said, "and told me that I must love the people even when they do not love me."

And that he did, explaining to all of you—and to us—how we should respect one another, how we can learn from one another, and, most of all, how we can rebuild our relationships with one another through simple gifts of kindness, honour, and—most of all—love.

It is love that I learned most from my dad.

Love of our people, the Anishinaabe, but also our Cree and Métis relations and, in fact, Indigenous communities and nations everywhere. Love of family—with particular respect to the gifts carried by children and Elders. Dad embodied this principle most of all. In fact, I remember many times he was invited to be the featured keynote speaker at some big event somewhere, and the event would start and Dad would be out in the hotel lobby or parking lot drinking coffee with someone or telling jokes to kids. Or he would be finding some reason to fill up and turn on the legendary bubble machine he kept in the back of his truck.

Love of our culture. Of course, I'm speaking about our traditional culture and, in particular, our ceremonies, which he attended and introduced us all to—always encouraging us to pick up our work and speak Anishinaabemowin—but I'm also talking about a *human* culture of dignity, respect, kindness, and generosity. While hardly perfect, Dad dedicated his life to being an ethical and good neighbour, friend, and relative. There are countless stories of Dad taking care of, helping, and working with people from all walks of life, all politics, and all faiths in an effort to create a culture of respect between all living beings—a value he learned from his studies of treaty, of Midéwiwin, and of humanity.

This is a love, after all, that embodies wisdom, respect, bravery, honesty, humility, and—perhaps most of all—truth.

Love is what he taught us right until the end of his time in this life.

Let me explain.

It's 2 a.m. and my turn with Dad.

My siblings are asleep in the next room, having spent the day moving our father to palliative care and visiting with him and so many others.

It's dark, quiet. Solemn.

I feel Dad's chest. His breaths are growing shorter. He shifts his body slightly to the left—a side he feels less pain from. I tell him it's me. He nods. He eases; his eyes are closed, but he is there.

Then, I do what he has been asking me to do since he got sick. What he did for his dad. I tell him the story of what happens to Anishinaabe people when they die—a part of our Creation story. If you ever get a chance to hear it, take it: it's one of the most remarkable, joyful, and brilliant stories about the miracle of love. I recite it to him again. I fight off tears, even though those are a part of the story, too.

Dad's breaths shrink. His face drains of pain. He is relaxed. Listening.

It's almost that time—the time when he will begin his next stage of life, his journey to our ancestors, and his beloved wife and life partner, in the west.

I wake my sisters, who join me and surround him.

I finish the story. I tell him, "I'll make the fire, Dad."

He nods, faintly, slightly, truly. For the last time in this life.

"Come to the fire, Dad. Look for it."

I tell him this because the first, and arguably most important, part of an Anishinaabe funeral—or, as we call it, an end-of-life ceremony—is the making of an ishkode or sacred fire. It's a fire that must be struck, fostered, and cared for near where the family cares for their relative over four days.

Like every sacred fire, nothing but good things must happen around it. Medicines and healthy wood must be the primary fuel. No garbage may be used in or around this warm, kind, and giving place.

A sacred fire is, in fact, a grand relation who cares for everyone who visits it.

A fire at an Anishinaabe end-of-life ceremony does more work than this, though. It is taught among Anishinaabe people that when a spirit leaves a body (also known as a life vessel), the transition is very disorientating and hard.

This makes sense, for a spirit and life vessel are one for a long time—especially for those who lived very rich lives, like a knowledge keeper, leader, and Elder. Just as a body gets used to being connected to a spirit, a spirit gets used to being connected to a body.

For the first while, especially during the initial stages after a spirit leaves their life vessel, they may not know what has happened, what to do, or where to go. In the spirit world, everything is different—some say everything is the opposite. It's a place where time, food, water, and life exist in a different way. Life is full of joy, meaning, and love, but in ways we have yet to know.

For instance, the daytime of the spiritual world—when spirits most often travel and move throughout Creation—is our nighttime. A relative's spiritual journey home after getting used to so much time in our world is not easy and requires a little bit of help.

This is where the fire comes in.

When a sacred fire is lit for an end-of-life ceremony, a transitioning relative's traditional name—the name the spiritual world uses to refer to a person's spirit—is spoken. All of Creation is informed that this fire is for that person's spirit. It is marked, a beacon representing where home is. This means a spirit always has a place to come back to, where they can see their family members, loved ones, and vessel.

Without the burden of uncertainty, a spirit is then free to travel throughout Creation, experiencing everything they loved in their life: the places, the moments, and the people.

And travel they do—over three nights.

For some, like my father, this meant he travelled very far and wide, and visited many, many people. If you are reading this, you're probably one of them. I hope you said hello. No matter how distant and deep a spirit travels, this fire marks a place for a spirit to rest, prepare, and hear instructions for the next step of its journey.

On the fourth day, the fire's work is done. There is new work for the spirit to do. It's time to travel to their other home. This is a place where the spirits of all those passed on exist and where a great feast awaits their arrival.

For my dad, this is the place where his grandparents, his parents and brothers, and the woman he loved so deeply, our mother, await him. For in the end, this story is about how love begets love.

What the Honourable Justice, Commissioner, and Senator Murray Sinclair leaves behind now is his immense, encompassing, and everlasting love for all of us. It is a duty, a standard, and a responsibility for all of us to live up to now. We must take up the work of caring for one another as he cared for us—so we can live in a future that is better than the one we inherited.

One time, in an interview, Dad was asked—as he often was—what people can do to create a better and more inclusive society. His answer, unsurprisingly, was about love—but it was also about what he had learned during his time with Granny Cate, his colleagues, his friends, and from the many places he travelled, danced, and shared stories and time, with all of us and with all of you. I leave you now with his words from a 1997 presentation at an Elders-policy makers-academics constituency group meeting in Quebec, truly his call to action:

> *Ultimately, no matter how we envision it, change rests with you, those of you who are here and ready to put in the hard work to do it. For change to happen, though, you have to commit personally, those of you who think this is important, to see this will happen.*
>
> *You have to go back to where you come from, your governments, your workplaces, your homes, and you have to go back Monday morning and send a*

memo or have a meeting or just sit and visit and make a commitment—professionally and personally. Imagine what a world looks like where all of us have medicines, food, and a safe place to live—not just a few but all of us, truly. Sometimes you will have to speak about this many times to many people because there are many who may doubt this is possible. But keep trying. Dream. Dream always because you have been given the gift to do that.

We have a lot of ground to cover, and we have a short time to do it. I want to be able to leave this life, this earth, thinking I have moved the conversation along a little bit, and I hope you will commit your life to the same thing, that when you are done whatever it is you do, you will feel that you have moved the conversation along a little bit. I hope these words I have shared with you have given you a little appreciation for how I feel about these things.

I do not pretend to have the answers. I sometimes feel I only have questions, but I do want you to know that I have strong feelings about this. A strong feeling about the importance of these issues in this day and age, and also a strong feeling about the important role each and every one of you is going to play, and the resolution of those changes. Because you all matter. All of us matter. Our elders matter. Our children matter. You matter. Making this world better will take all of us. Never forget that. Never forget that. Change will happen if the citizens of this country believe and make it happen. So, believe. Then, get up, do something about it. Don't just sit there. Get up.

Get up.

K'zaagin niibaabaa. I love you, Dad.

JOSHUA WHITEHEAD   *Shoot, Shovel, and Shut Up*[1]

I.

I am eulogiac.

I was first invited to Rideau Hall in 2016. I won the Governor General's
History Award for my poem "mihkokwaniy." The senses, overloaded.
Like the heated Valyrian knife of Rhaenyra Targaryen that foretells the
song of ice and fire—I too stood ablaze in glyph and syllabic. They tell
me that I sound ancient when I speak to you of the Algonquin.

Velvet. Oak. Teak. Cartilage.

What an exhibition to be enveloped within. There is a photo of my
mother and me wearing that same velvet, draped around the baroque—
such profundity twisted up in the knots of our smiles. In another photo,

[1] Also known as the 3-S Treatment as retaliation against an animal preying on livestock;
popularized form of settler nationalism and anti-Indigenous rhetorics regarding Colton
Boushie and most recently the 2022 Saskatchewan stabbings.

I'm standing in front of the portrait of Queen Elizabeth II. Pageant of class, hands in a prayerful stance. I have come to bury my grandmother. "Denied any history of their own, it was the fate of 'primitive peoples' to be dropped out of the bottom of human history in order that they might serve, representationally, as its support . . . the point at which human history emerges from nature."[2] Posited on this ledge of modernity and history, the Hall a tomb of conquest. A curation of story the nation tells itself to stratify. Decadent and profane. I might dare you to entomb me—which isn't so much a dare as it is the truth of imperial ideology. Would my grandmother be carried with such ferocity and grace to her death chamber among her ancestors as Elizabeth was? Who stood vigil at her autopsy table?

Find a bell jar to house the almonds of our amygdala.

"Shoot," he proclaims in bush and vigilante. pâskisikewin[3] might be the shot I take to gift the murdered a space of remembrance. A headstone is a luxury. "We hung our dead in trees."[4] Effigies of birch. "All the trees in the world are going to fall sooner or later. But not on us."[5] pâskîw[6] of the blanket of takwakin,[7] we are ready for our snow bath—the time for story and snag arrives.

---

[2] Tony Bennett's "The Exhibitionary Complex."
[3] The act of firing a shot/bullet; target practice.
[4] Emily Riddle's *The Big Melt*.
[5] Cormac McCarthy's *The Road*.
[6] S/he uncovers herself/himself.
[7] Autumn.

kisik,[8] look to her, I want for trees to fall upon us. Might this too be vigil? pahkihtin kimistik miyaw tâwikiskawêw nimistikwan[9]—bite into my bark the stories of revival. Crunch into the hardwood of this scaffold the prayers of sweat and stone. For all stones know a weeping song.

Immemorial memorial.

niya pâskinam wakîc pâskisikan ekwa nîyanân paskiswaw pakwâno-moniyaw âcimowinak.[10] masinahikâsiw.[11]

This is how I wrote a eulogy: you don't need to be godly to be goodly.

2.
September 6, 2021: my uncle is struck by a car and dies instantly.

June 15, 2022: my last remaining maternal uncle is found dead in his bed.

Both times I am in Toronto. Both times I am with a partner (a different one each time). Both times I let mourning engulf me. I climb the CN Tower. Atop its needle, I light a cigarette. Emblazed, I pour across the city core dreams of wild tobacco and sweet smoke. Become an arrow-head. Knocked, I bow into the sky and pierce the heart of a thunderbird. Which is not to say I am deadly in my musings. I want to touch the

[8] The sky.
[9] Your body tree falls down into me/my head.
[10] I turn the page upon the gun and we are cut free from white (man) history/stories.
[11] S/he is recorded.

thorax of god. Nestle in her bone cage. Cite creation in a thunderstorm.
Spill from caruncle and divine rallies for these losses.

I don't know if I see it all that often.
That we've become our forebearers' dreams?
I suppose we're walking contradictions.
And what beautiful metaphors we've become.

I want to find beauty in the world and translate that into joyful story-
ing. My published work up until this point in my life has become a
eulogy for the dead. My epigraphs a violent graphing. "Do you think
your fathers are watching? That they weigh you in their ledgerbook?
Against what? There is no book and your fathers are dead in the
ground."[12] I am here again for my touring of *Making Love with the Land*.
A materialized formulation of my mental warrings. I share story with
audience. It appears they have learned from this new story. And yet, I
am racked with anxiety. Struggle to catch my breath. Sweat on stage.
Pores too crying. A publication is meant to be celebratory, and I lament.
I find myself reading *The Road* again. I write into the margins—Papa do
you hear me too? Boy, might I take a turn at fathering?

I just want to be beautiful.
But you are. You already are. Look at you.
I don't mean beauty in the sense of skin.
I can feel the pain of your histories when you speak to me.
Why do you thank me for human decency?

[12] McCarthy, *The Road*.

I want to be a beautiful wreck site.

I want to be beautiful in the sense that when I come across a wound it emanates.

Like when pain becomes not a beacon but a blazing?

I want the hurt to see in me a tenacity that over defines the word "harmed."

I let his *you* become me: "Can you do it? When the time comes? When the time comes there will be no time . . . Hold him in your arms. Just so. The soul is quick. Pull him toward you. Kiss him. Quickly."[13] Such so, I have already done it. I have split the skull of nation with a rock and found naught but a book-to-tax reconciliation and my name as deduction. Cormac is a catharsis. The abysmal, greyed book is enlightening to me. I want to know why.

My body is a border between myself and the world, not a vehicle.

That is the problem.

3.

I am elegiac.

A BIPOC queer gives a land acknowledgement during Calgary Pride. I think he gives more of a land claim in all honesty. I am guest to a vogue ball—inside the history of Black queer NYC. The acknowledger orates, "We thank Indigenous people for sacrificing themselves." I am standing

---

[13] McCarthy, *The Road.*

in the background wearing a beaded red-hand medallion. I dissipate outside of history.

No power owns us. There is only the privilege of being with us.

Stop trying to sound like a writer and *write*.

I am romanticized by it too all the time. Do we ever move out of our monogamy with animating death as our fuelling desire? I guess for me as I've noted for you: it's been in my refusal to dance with death and to want to find intimacy and joy and love beyond the maw of desire masquerading as serration. If we eat one another like alpha predators then not much is left, in my opinion. This is why I feel I cannot inherit the tragedy of gay history; why it disbars me from its holograms. 1969 is my yesterday. I want my voice to reach back, at least a week, if not more. There isn't much echoing being done. The forests are all clear-cut. My queerness must mean more than vulturing a decayed and decades-old carcass. I wonder what other possibilities exist for us beyond being ghost and relic?

The "history of sexuality [i]s a 'history of western desire.'"[14]

Echo eulogia:
[mamihci]mowewin: a eulogy, to dignify, congratulate
[mâmihk]: downstream, down river

[14] Scott L. Morgensen's *Spaces Between Us: Queer Settler Colonialism and Indigenous Decolonization*.

[mâmihchi]: please him, make him proud
[mamihkowiw]: s/he is still bleeding

Silence hurts my ears. I find its presence in my proximity a harmful form of kinship. I am far too familiar with white noise in the quotidian. I crave the sounds of song and croak. My electricity stops working for an evening. I call my dog into the bed. I rest my head near his. He places paw upon head. Instinctively, he knows to pull me into his crook of leg and chest. The world is full of noise to him, this world and the fourth. His heartbeat is a welcomed song and I regress into a womb state.

God. Has anyone ever rested more wholly than when we were children in the backseat of a car at night, drifting off to the audible but imperceptible chatter of our parents' hushed voices?

Come and rest in this conciliatory symphony.

If you're reading this strange and unnatural note twenty or thirty years from now, you most likely have a third leg, and there's no such thing as body hair or nipples anymore, and the earth is scorched to shit, and the only people who have clean water are Elon Musk and Jeff Bezos, the villainous cretins, who somehow found a way to live to 156. Sweet jeezus, what a nightmare.

And speaking of wild shit, hundreds of years ago, when the Irish first got here, they came with these curious fables and folklore about beautiful, winged Fairies who live deep in the groves, but you never want to fuck with them or even their bundle of bushes. "Bad things will happen to you," the Irish say. "You lose all your money. Your pets will be savagely devoured by a pack of wolves, and then you're next."

Right. Have the Fairies been flushed out of their homes in the name of "progress" and capital greed yet? It's occurred to me that the worldwide, fat-cat corporate land rape would've reached such a vicious state in your epoch that nothing and nowhere is safe, not even those ancient groves, and that the Fairies are taking brutal revenge on the corpulent land rapists while the wolves gnaw on their faces.

By the way, has Big Foot trundled out of his bush yet? (Do white people still call him "Big Foot"?) I would imagine that the oil and gas asshats would've demolished their world by now too, subsequently setting off some Irish Fairy and Indigenous Big, Hairy People battle against the monstrous, human havoc—us.

And should all this come to pass, it would mean we, today, failed in our fight to protect the people, the land, the water, the four-leggeds, the swimmers, our winged relatives, and those otherworldly beings who have justifiably decided to keep a safe distance from our horrendous, homo sapiens, selfish fuckery.

But what the hell—I'm in a good mood at this moment, if you couldn't tell. My veins are full of caffeine and that ghost who moves my dishes and doesn't seem to know how to shut a fucking door is gone now. So, I'm going to hope none of that evil shit has happened to you in your time; that the Fairies are still cozy in their shaded groves; that the Big Hairy Ones have their feet up wherever the hell they hole up, and that you still have your nipples.

Indeed. And enough of all that. A huge thunderclap just shattered my kitchen windows, or at least that's what it sounded like. My dog is going completely sideways from the bang and my phone won't stop sending me nasty alerts about the rise of neo-Nazis in America and secret celebrity weddings in Las Vegas. "May you live in interesting times," the old Chinese proverb goes. And, hot damn, do we . . . pandemics, the irreversible baking of the planet, poisoned water, police brutality of brown and Black bodies, and taco trucks owned by guys named Chad and Skylar selling shitty carnitas for twenty-four bucks a pop. Madness, I tell you.

Well, I just turned thirty-nine, which means I'm staring down the barrel of the big 4-o. And, really, what wisdom can I impart upon you now that I've lived through this truly heinous shit-show circus for nearly four savage decades? Lo, I've got a few principles I live by on the daily, and perhaps you will, too: Never trust a Republican, especially white, radical Christian gun-humpers who say things like, "My family has always lived on this land" or anyone anywhere who gives a shit about spontaneous celebrity weddings in hovels like Las Vegas. Their skulls are rancid milk, and if you spend enough time around these bent heads as I, a reporter, do, you can smell their rotten intentions as soon as they walk in.

And I suppose the point of this screed is to encourage you to keep a weather eye for those with backwards, self-serving priorities. Yes. Avoid anyone who cares more about their right to own an AR-15 than an evil, constant barrage of murdered babies whose blood stains the American ground as well as GOP palms. Gawd, what an image: bloody palms. Reeking of rancid milk. And usually, a massive diesel truck shitting plumes of black smoke into the air with a Trump Now and Forever flag flapping in the back as they drive toward their next racist rally. They're easy to spot, even to the blind. But, again, if you're reading this twenty or thirty years from now, perhaps diesel trucks have been phased out along with sexting, walking, and people with peanut allergies. I imagine you, too, live in interesting times, and I'm sorry to say this, but I can't imagine things are going to get wildly better here in the US or Canada in the next one hundred or two hundred years. Think about it: Columbus and his lascivious sailors stumbled upon Turtle Island exactly 530 years ago, and even if their God, Jesus himself, came to defend the poor, the sick, and the hungry today, the Republican bent heads would probably beat him with a cross, string him up, and call him a "libtard, hippie, leftist, fucking Indian-lover."

Well, I think it's about time to bring this treatise to an end, which has clearly been an indictment on our widespread white, Christian, conservative penis problem. "We don't know who are the good ones and who are the bad ones," my Elder likes to say, "and that's the way it's been since they got here."

Now, more thunderclaps a'clappin'. My Great Dane has finally calmed down. After a heavy storm, when the skies go black and then clear, exposing the sun, and the ground glistens like a dance floor made of diamonds, you can almost hear the earth breathe. She likes to tell stories. And that's not just the psilocybin mushroom talking. That was Tuesday.

And the epilogue to this story is to never befriend the rich and the rotten, always have bail money squirrelled away for those days when the fuzz arrests you for defending the water, the land, and your inalienable Indigenous rights, and watch out for anyone who reeks of rancid milk while buying tacos from Chad and Skylar. Salud. Here's to the Fairies, to Big Foot, and to you—you poor, poor, beautiful bastard. Tokša akhé.

Simon Moya-Smith
Thursday, July 21, 2022
Santa Fe, New Mexico
a.k.a. Stolen Land

We need to decolonize our dreams.

Maybe this comes with the work of decolonizing our minds. But I worry that our dreams cannot wait for our conscious minds to undo all those centuries of colonial conditioning. That the choices we must make, collectively and individually, are too urgent for our current collective capacity for rational thought. It seems we are adrift from rationality. We need the power of our unconscious, of our unfettered imaginations, to meet this moment. Dreams arise when our soul and mind dance. We need them to dance to an old rhythm.

Dreaming outside the confines of colonial thought is something we all need to manifest, and quickly, for the time of colonial reality, and its dreams, are coming to an end. The evidence is all around us. Systems established by colonialism to serve its own master, capitalism, are in seizure or outright collapse. It's possible that by the time you read this, the largest empire the globe has ever known will have been finally, inevitably, thrown beyond democracy and into some form of authoritarian rule. If this hasn't come to pass yet, it is likely still imminent, or something else has happened that renders its coming moot.

What a depressing way to start a letter. But since this is what I think and feel in this moment, this is how we have to begin.

My instinct is to always write about hope, because how are we to face the coming times without it? Is it not my duty, and yours, to at least contribute hope? I'm all for hope, but not blind hope, not the sort of hope that fails to recognize just how large it needs to be.

It's daunting to write even in this moment. I just finished reading Baldwin again. And more Fanon before that. Dubois. bell hooks. John Trudell. Arthur Manuel, Angela Davis. They, and so many others, knew that this is where we'd end up, and they wrote so beautifully and powerfully in trying to guide us away from it—or rather, guide those who could change it.

But here we are, and here I am writing this letter, trying to imagine what they think.

Sadly, I only know what I think. And I think hope may be our final refuge. So we must take it, and from there, we fight.

Why fight? Because when cornered, that is all that is left to be done. If by now it's not clear that we are cornered, I wonder if it ever will be, just as the heating water is invisible to the lobsters already in the pot.

When I consider all that is happening, and total collapse provides a list of failures far too long for the confines of any reasonable letter, I am again and again driven to the same conclusion. That these things are collapsing as the result of a systemic reshaping of communities and of a distorted meaning of community, one that's rendered humans incapable of stopping what's happening and has us instead accelerating toward the end.

It was during the Covid pandemic that, to me, it became crystal clear that the societies we currently live in, at least in this part of the colonized world, are not actual communities at all. That the systems constructed to support them do not actually have community at the centre. How else can we explain how we so quickly gave up trying to protect one another from a contagious and potentially deadly virus, and so quickly decided individualism was the solution, that economic activity supersedes all, including human life?

Of course, we have long had ample evidence that these were the choices that would be made, as these places were built on the exact same calculus: that some human lives should be sacrificed for the economic stability and growth of others. It's the barbaric bargain built into capitalism and its ravenous offspring colonialism from their inception, and it's an equation that has clearly reached far. My family knows of this math all too well. Yet still, in the early days, there was a sense that maybe we would face this together, to care for and look after one another in a way that suggested real community. But that quickly gave way to profit protection, then outright profiteering. Our governments quickly revealed their corporate centres.

What seemed like a moment to reorient ourselves to community instead yielded a desire to return to a normal that was always lost. What we have seen and will see more of is a regression away from much of the progress made in the previous two generations.

It seems to me that it's because they have commerce instead of community at their centre that so many of this society's systems are collapsing at the same time. Those that should guide us in these moments—government, health, education, media, even organized religion—are afflicted with the same sickness, and so are unable to react as even the humans that populate them might want to. This only further deepens the issue, as people lose faith in these systems and become increasingly unable, unwilling, or incapable of facing the real affliction.

Remember those first few weeks of the pandemic? It was scary. There was a run on essentials at grocery stores; people were scared. We didn't know anything, but were desperate to know everything.

Then there were images of solidarity, people taking care of one another. In my neighbourhood, people hung signs and tied ribbons on trees to thank healthcare workers. There were images of nature returning when the commerce slowed, whales and birds being spotted where they hadn't been in some time.

It was that moment when we had a chance to listen. Listen to what the world was telling us. That we needed to slow down, maybe even stop. That we needed to remember the importance of gathering, of sharing literal space together, and how central to human existence that is. To allow us the space to fully witness what we have wrought, to take measure and reassess. We have so little space to do that now, to truly sit with where we find ourselves. I increasingly think we are kept busy so that we may not ponder, so that we may not dream.

So many are desperate for the sense of community that has been stripped from colonial settler states that people begin to form community in unhealthy ways and means. Because even a sick community provides something that these places don't. A sense of belonging. A sense of shared existence. Even if it's an unhealthy one.

They find it in conspiracies that explain the failures they see around them in a way that allows them to place blame not on the system they trusted in, but rather on forces that seek to somehow pervert it, or corrupt it from its true purpose, which they believe is to secure them.

But the system, if it was ever designed to serve humans, stopped doing that a while ago—around the time it became clear it was actually going to have to serve *everyone*, something it was never built to do. When faced with the possibility of sharing, those who hoard would rather destroy what they prize than allow others to have it. After all, the value only goes up if there's less to go around. Deprivation and scarcity are necessities in this system. Someone has to go without.

But in the pandemic, suddenly this disparity became stark to more people. Even those who share racial identities saw that the hoarding was not for them. The system revealed its true hunger, one that cannot be satiated. And instead of staring the system in its eyes, many become distracted by the conspiracy in the corner. They needed to avoid realizing they believed the lie. They bought the false promise at the heart of it all. The promise that if you looked the other way while others were brutalized, your day would come, and you'd be lifted above the brutality.

But that day hasn't come. And instead, the lie at the heart of the promise is shining brighter. That's why so many want to remain asleep. It's why being awake has suddenly become a pejorative—because the dream promised has been shattered.

We are told, in the face of so much information, so much truth, that we should be ignorant. That we should not learn our history. I have never understood the notion that ignorance is bliss, until now, when so many want to be blissful.

These nations are too juvenile to face their actions, so they ban the books that teach it, and stop people from speaking it. And then they call it freedom.

They had their own writers telling them this was coming: Orwell, Huxley, Butler. But do we read anymore?

So, we get convoys for freedom during a pandemic, where basic community health measures—something functioning communities hold close—are equated to oppression. And because those protesting come largely from the population these colonies were meant to serve, the powers that be are at a loss at how to enforce order, despite demonstrating their prowess at it anytime protestors come from populations these places are meant to extinguish.

People need community, so they're going to find it, or they will manufacture it.

So what we must do is rebuild the very understanding of community that we seem to have collectively lost. Is this the prophecy my people speak of? When the world will turn back to us so we may all learn how to live together again?

It's long overdue that we resolve issues created by the systems we have become beholden to, namely poverty and houselessness. These are not natural outcomes; rather, they are imposed ones, and we should stop imposing them. We need to see a massive reinvestment and reorganization of our health systems. One that centres the whole human and reflects the interconnected nature of our health and the environments we exist in.

We need to invest in spaces where we can physically gather safely, without the need to spend money. Where can we ever gather now that our simple presence isn't part of someone's business plan? Certainly not social media. Maybe the library or a park? But those are not universal spaces.

All of this requires such an inversion, such a dream, that I worry we can't conjure it. But we must. We must break free of the limited space granted our dreams now. Dreams about becoming rich or powerful? Why? To escape. Or dreams of holding on to those things, or even expanding them? Why? To escape.

Escape what? I've asked myself. What is it we're all trying to escape?

We deny our own humanity whenever we deny someone else's, and that's what these systems and structures are built upon. They are designed to disguise the network of relations that humanity relies on to exist. This allows for the excessive exploitation that has brought us here. We are valued for what we produce, not for our very being, our blunt humanity.

Can we dream our way back to ourselves? Systems change, social justice, decolonization, they all end in the same place: becoming comfortable with our human selves and the weakness that is inherent there. Being humble in the face of that truth, so that we may once again find right relations with our kin—human and otherwise—with the land and sky, and, of course, with ourselves.

I took my dream catcher down the other day. I want the dreams to flood in unfettered. Even the nightmares. I need them now. I hope you are dreaming of what should be and also what simply is. I hope we are all dreaming, so that we may find one another. And that through finding ourselves and rebuilding the notion of community, our dreams, and ourselves, can be truly free to dance.

In love and solidarity,
Jesse

CINDY BLACKSTOCK

*To My Ancestors,
My Contemporaries,
and Those Who Have
Not Yet Joined Us*

For my ancestors, let me begin with a simple but sincere thank you.

Thank you for all you have done, for all you have shared, for passing down the best of who you are. Thank you for all your sacrifices and for laying the roots from which change can grow. I am so grateful to have been able to draw on the wisdom and the lessons you have shared with each generation that has come after yours, as we navigate this world.

Doing so is more than just a privilege; it is a duty. And yet, while we are fortunate to be able to turn to such vast amounts of wisdom, it is disheartening—yet not at all surprising—that long after you have left us, we still find ourselves taking up the same fight as you.

To my contemporaries, one thing I continue to emphasize is the connection between the systems of the past and those of the present, the events and experiences you've lived through and the ones that continue to impact First Nations, Inuit, and Métis children, families, and communities today. Too often these connections are obscured, not by a matter of chance, but as part of a direct strategy upon which governments rely to continue their ongoing pattern of discrimination. And as you know better than anyone, they are quite good at this—they have had centuries of practice.

But despite being told to accept the discrimination as a fact of life, we know from the past that it is important to act on the contemporary injustices because they are solvable.

This is where we look to the courage and the commitments of the current generations. The reality is clear; we have our work cut out for us. We have made important strides, but there is still much left to do to ensure that First Nations, Inuit, and Métis kids can grow up safe, healthy, and at home with their families. At the same time, I am especially grateful for all the caregivers who looked after the First Nations kids who couldn't stay at their homes, but could at least stay close by, surrounded by community.

The first step is to learn about the injustices. Spirit Bear and I are always so thrilled to see classes of young people taking up reconciliation campaigns and committing to the Truth and Reconciliation Commission of Canada's Calls to Action—especially by focusing on the calls that directly affect children and youth. We are grateful to the educators who have made a point to help bring truth and reconciliation to their classrooms and impart a sense of justice upon the current generation of warriors. To the kids who are committed to learning and acting, I say keep going! We need you to continue to help us stand up for what's right.

Kids have no trouble distinguishing between what's right and what's wrong—it's one of their gifts. Things tend to get a bit cloudier for adults. Although today's kids can benefit from educators who are committed to helping them learn about truth and reconciliation and Canada's history, older generations weren't always so lucky. We all have an obligation to educate ourselves, because we were often denied the opportunity to learn about these experiences in school. But that lack of knowledge is what has allowed discrimination to persist. How can you fight against an injustice when you don't know that it exists?

The Government of Canada relies on the assumption that most of the population is unaware of their ongoing discrimination against First Nations, Inuit, and Métis kids. When the headlines die, so do the children, and the antidote is that public interest doesn't die.

For those who are not yet with us, please know that just as our ancestors did for us, we are fighting to leave the world in a better place so that you can grow up knowing that you are supported, cared for, valued, and loved and are never made to feel otherwise by those in power.

When residential school Survivors gifted us with the Calls to Action, they made sure that the first five of the ninety-four addressed child welfare so that their grandchildren wouldn't have to go through the same things that they did. We commit to continuing to act in that same spirit so that, hopefully, you can grow up safe and healthy, get a good education, and be proud of who you are without struggle.

We are so proud to see what good you will bring to the world, what gifts you'll share with those around you, as the generation that our ancestors dreamt of.

I want to begin by acknowledging one of my personal heroes, Murray Sinclair. I have held so much respect and admiration for the late Chancellor Senator Sinclair. Murray moved the needle forward for all Indigenous peoples, and the immense scope of his work has changed this country. His work as the chief commissioner of the Truth and Reconciliation Commission (TRC) brought forward the difficult truths of the residential school experience to Canadians who had been taught very little—if anything—about this dark chapter of the colonial project.

The TRC report brought focus to my own art and charged it with an urgency to communicate our truths no matter how difficult or painful they are to look at. Empowered by the weight of this commission, I believed that if I could bring the truths from this report to life in my paintings, they might reach an audience more effectively than reports or news feeds ever could.

A few years ago, I made a controversial painting that stirred up a lot of complicated feelings and strong reactions from the mainstream but also within the Indigenous community. It was an allegorical painting that confronted violence against Indigenous women and Two-Spirit people. There was a lot of debate on social media, and Murray asked everyone who was feeling hard emotions about it to pause and consider the message, and then he offered an incisive interpretation of the work. He readily agreed that it was disturbing to look at—he said he never wanted to see it again—but that that was the point. That experience and listening to our communities' perspectives gave me lots to reflect on, but it was Murray's words, and his commitment to looking at hard truths, that helped me refocus.

Around the same time, there was much debate in the country about what to do with public statues memorializing colonial leaders. Murray again asked the Indigenous community to pause and suggested that maybe instead of vandalizing and tearing them down, we should build monuments to our own people. I took inspiration from his words again and began painting a series of portraits titled *Shining Stars*: large-scale portraits of my personal heroes in the Indigenous community—young and old, activists, artists, academics, knowledge keepers—to canonize us into the art history of this continent that tried to erase us.

I've been an artist my whole life. There was never anything else that I wanted to do. I am fortunate that my artistic identity was solidified when I was a precocious child at the age of four or five by my parents and extended family. A doting Cree great-grandmother—my granny Caroline Everet, born in 1875, who died at the age of a hundred when

I was ten years old—was my first attentive audience. She only spoke to me in her beautiful old Cree. Later as a professional artist, I came to realize that my strong attraction to the late nineteenth century, in both art and history, was very personal; Granny was my living link to the history of the Red River area and the period of the signing of the numbered treaties. Often I have thought about her experience as a ten-year-old girl when the uprising of 1885 unfolded a few miles from her family's community at St. Peter's, Manitoba.

One of her thirteen children—only three of whom survived to adulthood—was my grandmother Elizabeth Monkman, a survivor of the notorious Brandon residential work camp for children—I can't call it, or any of them, "school." Grandma applauded my violin recitals and encouraged me as an artist. And of course my parents proudly displayed my crayon drawings on the fridge or made Christmas cards out of them. My family never placed limitations on me. I had been given a gift, a strong belief in myself. Even though we didn't have much and went through some very tough times as a result of the colonial project—that took a huge toll on many generations of my family and those of almost every other Indigenous person I know—my grandmothers and parents made me feel as though my art had as much value as anyone else's in the world. I belonged.

As an artist in my twenties, I was influenced by a wide range of artists, from the old masters to the abstract expressionists, and by Indigenous artists a generation ahead like Fritz Scholder, Jane Ash Poitras, Joane Cardinal-Schubert, Robert Houle, and others. With these disparate influences, my twenties and part of my thirties were spent making abstract paintings. I eventually abandoned abstraction when I realized that this cryptic language of painting was failing to communicate the themes that were becoming more urgent to me personally: colonized sexuality and the larger themes of colonization that still continue to have devastating impacts on my family and my community. I wanted to reach the widest audience possible and found that the representational vocabulary of history painting would allow me to connect with everyone in all communities across these lands we call Canada, and the world.

As my work evolved over the years, I wanted to communicate the beauty and depth of knowledge found in Cree ways of knowing, but also speak truthfully to my contemporary urban experience. Over two decades ago, I created an alter ego, Miss Chief Eagle Testickle, who came to life inside my history paintings to disrupt colonial narratives. Her journey from the dawn of life to the present day, stitched into Cree cosmology with the help of four Cree language speakers and knowledge keepers—Dr. Belinda Daniels, Floyd Favel, Dr. Keith Goulet, and Gail Maurice—is told in her two-volume memoir, co-written by long-time collaborator and dear friend Gisèle Gordon.

My art has tackled difficult subjects head-on with brutal honesty, imagination, and a good dose of the sass and humour that was always a part of any Cree gathering and is embedded in our stories. I have made art about the children's work camps that were designed to assimilate us, strip us of our languages and cultures, and turn us into a servant class on our own land. The meagre education our ancestors and Elders received was not intended to elevate them to the middle or governing classes—rather, it was just enough education to provide the settler population with clerks and servants.

I have made art that speaks to the impact of the colonial project that endures in many insidious forms. There are more Indigenous children living as wards of the child welfare state today than those who were forced to attend the work camps. Disproportionate numbers of our men and women fill Canadian federal and provincial prisons and penitentiaries—up to ninety percent in some provincial prisons. Boil water advisories are ongoing in our communities; our waters are polluted by tailing ponds, poisoned from the endless extractions of oil and gas on our lands. The violence against us, against our missing and murdered women and Two-Spirit people, continues. Why do I create art that looks at these dark chapters? It's a way for me to process and heal for my own personal journey first, and then to also validate and authorize into the canon of art history the experiences of Indigenous people across this continent who have been erased from art history.

I had the privilege and opportunity to engage with Canadian audiences from coast to coast with two nationally touring solo exhibitions of my art from 2007 to 2018. I personally engaged with many thousands of university-educated people across Canada, a shocking number who told me over and over again, "We just didn't know, we were never taught anything about this..."

I was confronted with the fact that millions of North American settlers, immigrants, and visitors had graduated universities across this continent knowing little if anything about Indigenous truths, nor the complexities of our languages, cultures, or historical or contemporary experiences. Many successive governments since Confederation, conspiring with the church, concealed their crimes of genocide and made sure these truths were omitted from school curricula, from grade school to university.

Why isn't the report published by the Truth and Reconciliation Commission ten years ago included on every syllabus? Why aren't Indigenous languages taught in every university? Why aren't *we* taught our own languages and local dialects that were stolen from our parents and ancestors in every school and university? So much knowledge is embedded in our languages. Why aren't you taught the sciences in our ways of knowing? Have you made efforts to engage with the science deeply embedded in Indigenous ways of knowing such as astronomy, weather patterns, botany, and the study of medicinal plants?

To paraphrase Niigaan Sinclair, our creation stories are not legends or myths but scientific theories. You can find our stories—often rewritten by non-Indigenous authors—in the fiction section, or worse, in the children's literature section, as if they're some sort of second-tier Disney-like set of whimsical tales. Indigenous knowledge—found in the stories we tell, the songs we sing, and the actions we perform—is, first and foremost, science. The fact is that Indigenous peoples had to understand the world before they could talk about it. In other words, we are scientists before we are storytellers or artists.

My friend Dr. Leroy Little Bear teaches that Indigenous science is about relationships while Western science is about taxonomy and measurement.

I encourage you to improve your relationships with us. Listen to us. If the Indigenous people of the world are not well, neither are you. We are like the canary in the coal mine. You need us and our knowledge for rebalancing this world for our collective future. We speak our truths, but it's up to you to do the hard work now.

To remind you, we didn't need you. We existed here for many tens of thousands of years before you arrived, needing our help, which—in community after community—we largely gave to you. You still need us. We understood that the treaties we made—the ones that you and your ancestors benefitted from—meant that we entered into kinship with you and agreed to share this land.

I encourage you to honour the legacy of Murray Sinclair, as I have in my own work. Take inspiration from his leadership, his love for all Canadians, and his generosity. He believed deeply in the power of education and spent a great part of his life bringing our truths forward to educate you. It is now up to you to heed those Calls to Action in the TRC report and to create more space for us Indigenous people in our shared future together.

There's a drawer full of notebooks below my writing desk. There isn't an empty page within them. The pages are occupied by my father's thoughts on education or Indigenous identity, reconciliation and the path to healing, memories he'd recalled of his youth, or quotes that helped guide his work. I am only one, but I am one. I cannot do everything, but I can do something. What I can do, I ought to do. I interviewed my father several times in 2019, the year he died. I recorded them. They live in a folder on my computer. It's 2022 now, and there are days when I miss him as though he died only yesterday. I take out his notebooks on those days and read through them, searching for something new. I listen to our interviews. I skip through my questions and focus on his answers. He still teaches me.

The other day he told me, "In terms of looking at the future, we, as the upcoming grandparents, have a responsibility to look at seven generations from where we are and to look into the future. We want to look back and see what happened. We want to experience what's happening here and now. But we want to look forward to the future and develop a vision that will help, give us hope, and give young people hope, in terms of what it is they want to look forward to."

What kind of future do we want to look forward to?

I'm forty-five years old, an odd age where I'm not quite sure whether I'm young or old. I got an email recently from a university student writing a thesis that included my work, and they wanted to ask me a couple of questions. Offhanded, they mentioned that they'd met me previously. I'd come to speak to their school when they were in elementary.

Okay, I'm old.

I'd spoken to their school about the Indian Residential School System and the pathway to reconciliation. It was around the time I wrote *7 Generations* and *Sugar Falls*. Hearing this made me think of my experience in school and what I'd learned about Indian Residential Schools. Of course, I'd learned nothing. Canada has a track record of ignoring stuff that involves colonialism and its impacts. That's why, when presented with a scathing report on the deaths of children at Indian Residential Schools in the early twentieth century, they put their effort into destroying the report writer's career rather than trying not to let more kids die. I graduated from Kelvin High School and had no idea that down the street, about a ten-minute walk away, there was a former Indian Residential School where children were physically, sexually, and mentally abused. What a massive failure on multiple levels that history could be so blatantly ignored.

We can't change the past, but we can learn from it. We have to learn from it. We cannot know where we're going or where we want to go without first knowing where we've been and how we got to where we are today.

I hope that's not too confusing. It's taken me a long time to rectify the failures of my experience in school within the context of Indian Residential School history. I took a Native Studies course at university taught by a non-Indigenous instructor who didn't know what bannock was, which should have been a red flag for me, and not once did Residential Schools come up. So, the problem extended beyond elementary and secondary school.

I'm an intergenerational survivor of the Indian Residential School System. My grandmother attended Norway House Indian Residential School in the 1920s and 30s. She died in 1985 without having shared anything about her experience, short of mentioning to one family member that it had made her sad to have her hair cut and to my mother that she'd had a sister who died at school. In the 1980s, survivors weren't openly sharing their experiences, and the stories not told are a history lost. The best I can do to learn about what my grandmother may have experienced is to research Norway House Indian Residential School. I have done a great deal of research on the Indian Residential School System in various ways to circumvent the absence of knowledge in my formative years. This has equipped me to do a few things.

Early in my career, it helped me focus my work; I wanted every book I wrote to have intrinsic educational value and for that value to be connected to Indigenous people, cultures, communities, languages, histories, and contemporary issues. The priority was writing literature that educated youth about Indian Residential School history, something teachers could use in the classroom as a resource. I looked back on my childhood experience and didn't want one more child to graduate from high school without any knowledge about a system that profoundly impacted Indigenous people and this country. Becoming well-versed in Indian Residential School history and its impacts, being an intergenerational survivor, ensured that I could write a compelling story and answer difficult questions when visiting classrooms.

You have to know the history well enough so that you can talk about it accurately and appropriately but also so that you can answer the difficult questions kids will have. The focus has to be on kids. They are positioned, more than anybody else, to create positive change and lead us on the path toward reconciliation. A simple reason would be that they have the benefit of time. They simply have more of it to walk the path than adults do.

But it's more.

We were raised with barriers we need to break down before laying a foundation of truth. In high school, I was afraid to play basketball in the North End of Winnipeg because I was afraid of other Indigenous people. I believed they were violent, poverty-stricken addicts who were in gangs and would beat the shit out of me if they got the chance. How confusing and shameful that I was one of them. This perception was developed by stereotypes, misrepresentations, and a lack of education. (I did play basketball in the North End, and guess what? I was never beaten up.)

Walls that had been constructed needed to be shattered before anything else could happen in my journey toward self-acceptance and healing. A personal reconciliation. Nothing earth-shattering led me out of the dark and into the light. I got to know my father. I asked him questions, and he answered them. He gave his answers in the form of stories grounded in truth, from lived experiences. Against barriers like the ones I had, that sort of truth is a wrecking ball. It's a long process that many Canadians are just starting, but it's a process that enables us to build something new on a stronger foundation. Children do not have those barriers.

I used to say that children don't see colour, but I've come to believe, after meeting tens of thousands of children throughout my career, that this isn't accurate. They aren't colour-blind. They see their differences. They just don't give a shit. That is unless we make them give a shit. It's ironic. Parents are at the heart of most instances of banned literature, often because they're concerned that, for example, reading about a gay character might somehow, I guess, make their child gay. Or that reading about Indian Residential Schools or systemic racism is something children aren't ready for. But it's not the books that indoctrinate children; it's adults who either don't know any better, have never learned any better, or are simply ignorant and hateful.

We need to ensure that our children are better than us. That takes effort. It takes self-reflection, a willingness to listen and learn, and a recognition that it's not good enough for this country to be great for specific people instead of all. That we can't call ourselves a First World country when thousands of Indigenous people don't have access to clean drinking water. The problem doesn't go away if we pretend it's not there.

When I first started writing about the Indian Residential School System, when that university student was in elementary school, I travelled to schools in Manitoba and later across Canada to present my work to kids and discuss the history and its impacts. Back then, if I asked a group of kids—a classroom or an entire assembly—how many knew about Indian Residential Schools, very few would have put up their hands. I know because often I did that very thing. That was about thirteen years ago. Since then, we've seen the Truth and Reconciliation Commission of Canada and its widely ignored (by the Canadian government, at least) Calls to Action and a renaissance of Indigenous literature that has focused on reclaiming our stories and educating Canadians through them. The growth of published stories that feature Indigenous characters is gradual but assured. According to a study conducted by the Cooperative Children's Book Center in the US, out of over 3,000 children's books published in 2015, the representation of Indigenous characters was 0.9 percent. The study was repeated in 2018, and although other marginalized groups saw a moderate increase in representation, Indigenous characters clawed their way to a round number of 1.0 percent. In my experience, the publishing landscape in Canada reflects that of the landscape in the United States. So, Indigenous characters are vastly under-represented in children's literature. I suspect that if the same study had been carried out in Canada, the number in 2018 might have been higher than 1.0 percent. But not by much. How remarkable, then, that from week to week, the bestselling books in

Canada are populated by Indigenous literature. Publishers are beginning to recognize that not only do our books have intrinsic value, but putting them out into the world is profitable. Capitalism, am I right?

Fast forward thirteen years. If the Canadian government has continued to fail Indigenous people, as every government has since Confederation, segments of the population have been doing their part. Teachers and librarians have embraced their role in leading kids on the path toward reconciliation by working to realize Calls to Action specific to education. Call to Action 62(i) reads: "We call upon the federal, provincial, and territorial governments, in consultation and collaboration with survivors, Aboriginal peoples, and educators, to make age-appropriate curriculum on residential schools, Treaties, and Aboriginal peoples' historical and contemporary contributions to Canada a mandatory education requirement for Kindergarten to Grade Twelve students." The TRC Final Report was released in 2015. Over the last seven years, for the most part, with some exceptions in Alberta and Ontario, either in isolated incidents or province-wide, kids have been learning about Indian Residential Schools at all grade levels. And it's been working.

In mid-September 2022, I visited a school in Winnipeg ahead of the second National Day for Truth and Reconciliation. It was the first large assembly I'd presented for since the COVID pandemic shut the world down. Walking to the front of the stage, I was greeted by a sea of orange shirts and compassionate, committed teachers and educational leadership. The school's principal emotionally and powerfully discussed his journey to identity and reconciliation, and then I was introduced to the student body by two exceptional young Indigenous students. You could hear a pin drop as they dared to speak in front of almost four hundred of their peers. That alone showed that things had changed; they weren't hiding from who they were. They welcomed me in Cree, handed me tobacco, and publicly embraced the beauty of who they were unreserved. Before anything else, I asked all the kids, "Who here knows about Indian Residential School history?"

Every single kid in that gymnasium put a hand up. This was a recognition of the past. An expression that every one of those kids could articulate a complex history at their level. A Kindergarten student would have a different thing to say about it than a Grade Six student, but that's how it should be. Recognition of their role on this path we are walking together came from my second question.

"Who here would educate me about the history if I didn't know?"

When We Were Alone was published in 2016. It was the first picture book that educated children in Kindergarten or Grade One about Indian Residential Schools (although kids of all ages have read it often). One of the first classes I visited to read and discuss the book was a Grade One class in Calgary. The kids were primarily white, and none of them were Indigenous. I read the book to them, talked about it, and fielded their questions. It went well. After the class ended, the teacher pulled me aside to tell me a story. The week previous, she'd read the book to the kids in preparation for my arrival. The next day, a parent approached her and asked, "What did you read my kid?" The teacher was nervous that the parent might be upset she'd read my book to the kids, considering it was a complex subject for young learners. She showed the parent a copy of *When We Were Alone*. The parent looked it over for a minute, then said, "I have to tell you. I'd never learned about residential schools before, and my kid taught me last night."

If you want to know what reconciliation looks like, that's a pretty good example. To the question, "Who here would educate me about the history if I didn't know?" almost every child threw their hand into the air. On the heels of the discovery of 1,148 (never round up or down a number like this) unmarked graves at three locations across Canada—Kamloops Indian Residential School (215), Marieval Indian Residential School (751), and St. Eugene's Mission School (182)—a rally was organized at the Manitoba Legislature urging the country to cancel Canada Day. What was there to celebrate? The majority of Canadians, aside from Indian Residential School denialists, had come to realize what Indigenous people already knew: the Indian Residential School System was an act of genocide (whether the government admits it or not). It was not, as Carolyn Bennett, former minister of Crown-Indigenous Relations, said: a terrible mistake. Mistakes are not made deliberately. If I tell you that I'm going to punch you in the face, then I punch you in the face, I can't say afterwards that punching you was a terrible mistake. Canada aimed to kill the Indian in the child. They killed thousands of children. They refused to stop killing children when they were told outright that children were being killed. They cannot then say "Whoops." The attitude of the Canadian government is exactly this: Justin Trudeau knelt at an unmarked grave with a teddy bear for a fucking photo op. Meanwhile, his government spent millions fighting a decision that awarded survivors compensation for the hell they endured while attending Indian Residential Schools.

On the way to the rally on July 1, 2021, all five of our kids in tow, my wife heard of a girl named Willa selling lemonade to raise money for Indian Residential School survivors. We stopped there and, like many Winnipeggers, paid a lot of money for glasses of lemonade (it was a "pay what you can" sale). Willa raised $1,010 and split the donations evenly between Mama Bear Clan and the Indian Residential School Survivors Society. In an Instagram post, her mother wrote: "Willa was deeply upset by the discovery of mass unmarked graves at residential school sites. She felt so helpless and confused. I'm very proud of her for deciding to step into action. She continues to teach me."

By educating children, we are carrying out one of the most important roles adults have on the path to reconciliation. In Willa's case, she had been taught history and its impacts, which equipped her to do something meaningful. She was upset by what had happened but knew that being upset was not enough. I'm certain that thousands upon thousands of Canadians were upset at the news that unmarked graves had been discovered. After all, we're people who, I like to believe, care for one another. We're empathetic creatures, us human beings. But to be frank, being upset doesn't change a thing. Willa knew about the past, saw what was happening today, and decided that she wanted to play a role in ensuring that things were different tomorrow. So, she set up a lemonade stand.

We are all capable of doing something to contribute as we journey toward reconciliation. There is no excuse for not knowing the history; the books are out there, in classrooms, libraries, and bookstores. Not just about Indian Residential Schools, but also about this country's colonial history and the systems and policies designed to push Indigenous people to the margins of society. I've always thought it was funny (not funny) how the governments of this country have done whatever they can to beat us away with a stick while asking us, at the same time, to assimilate. Just look at the pass system. It was racial segregation. Starting in 1886, and as a way to prevent another Northwest Resistance, Indigenous people required a signed pass to leave their reserve. They were told where they could go and when they were to return.

There is no excuse for not knowing what is happening today and how it relates to our history. The genocide of Indigenous women, girls, and Two-Spirit People. The overrepresentation of Indigenous people in the criminal justice system. How Gerald Stanley, a middle-aged white man, could be acquitted by an all-white jury for shooting Colten Boushie, a young Indigenous man, in the head (and, in the end, receive a $3,900 fine for improperly storing a firearm). How Joyce Echaquan could die in a hospital bed in Quebec while two employees, including a nurse, made fun of her. She was "only good for sex." She was "stupid as hell." That there are more Indigenous children in the foster care system today than those in Indian Residential Schools at their peak. Our children make up almost sixty percent of all children in care. There is an inextricable link between the past and the present. Knowing the past and understanding that link gives us the ability to improve how things are today and tomorrow. Whatever is in your capacity to do, you ought to do. Teach yourself, teach a child, and watch this country change.

What's your lemonade stand?

Cedar

DAVID TREUER   *A Letter to My Brother*
                                     on His Fifty-Fifth Birthday

Dear Anton,

This letter, written on the 250th anniversary of our country's birth
(and—who knows?—maybe five hundred years after the birth of our
tribal nation, surely millennia after the birth of our culture) is, I have
to admit, hard to write. Not because writing is hard. It's not. Rather,
it's difficult, sometimes, to speak to you. It is hard to write to you, too,
because (and there is probably no easy way to say this—though it's
certainly more difficult to hear it) you are considerably softer than I.
Don't mistake me. Please understand: this isn't a bad thing. You are
softer in the sense that you've held on to your innocence a lot longer
than I have. You wear it on your face and in how you walk and how you
stand. It animates the energy with which you attack life itself, the life
you've imagined for yourself, for our children, and for our people. I don't
know where your softness comes from. It didn't come from our mother.
And it didn't come from our father for that matter. It's just something
that is true about you. I'm for better or worse (and between you and
me I'm leaning toward worse) harder. But this means I'm also more

brittle, more prone to breakage. Like rice that has been roasted and jigged when it was too green. Only good for soup.

Our mother (I don't need to tell you!) was something of a force. She grew up hard: a rez girl who did without running water and electricity and kindness and affection, but who went on to become someone in the world. Despite how she grew up and what she managed to achieve—or because of it—she, too, was by the end ready to break. She did, though not all at once. Well, she is dead now, and while she was alive I think she had a terrible life. She suffered the loss of all her siblings except one, and most of her cousins, and the loss, in ways large and small, of her sense of safety, which is to say, the sense of her self. She became, toward the end, a bitter person. Life for her was a complicated poison and, at the same time, a confusing antidote to that poison. However, through it all, somewhat miraculously, she had the strength (and I'd like to know where she got it!) not to believe what white people said about her. She was not, and never was, a "Nob" or a "savage" or a "dirty Indian." She was not, because she believed she was not, worthless. And although the source of your innocence may be something of a mystery to me, the fact that you, like our mother, do not subscribe to what white people have to say about us is clearly part of your matrilineage. Neither you nor our children exhibit that bitterness. You carry within you the same belief: that you are worth something, and that life owes you nothing less than its full expression. That she passed down the one thing and not the other makes me glad.

You are one year older than I am. This means quite a few things. It means that we grew up together, of course. And that we shared everything—experiences, things, feelings. When I look up from these words into the room of the past you are always in it. And when you look up you probably see me, too. Anyway, I watched you grow up just as you watched me. I watched you learn to walk, and you helped me with my first steps. I saw you off on your first day of school. You accompanied me on mine. I was there, by your side, as you learned and grew, and you were by mine. I watched you, first as a toddler and then as a boy and, finally, as a man come into the world and into yourself. And you did the same for me. I have never loved anyone else for as long or can understand anyone else as well as I think I understand you. When this is the case, as James Baldwin points out, "you gain a strange perspective on time and human pain and effort."

I tell our kids—often enough to cause their eyes to roll—that this is true for them as well. Lovers and partners, parents and friends, all of them, come . . . and then they will eventually go. But your brothers and sisters (and I have been referring to your kids and my kids as "our kids" because, for us, cousins are the same as siblings) are forever. We were, and still are, effectively twins. Although English is a language I am happy to wield, feel lucky to write in, and take great pride in bending to my purposes, it doesn't quite convey the full dimensions of that fact. Ojibwemowin does much better. Niizhoodenhyag. As you know, that's our word for twins. And as you know, "niizhoo" means two and "de" means heart. Two hearts. To be a twin is to be two-hearted. And while that may best describe us it doesn't mean that we are alike. Far from it. And that makes me glad. You are much kinder than I am. The world hasn't managed to beat that out of you.

You were born in Washington, DC, not long after our parents miscarried their first baby on the Beltway—our mother bleeding in her seat and our father frantically looking for an exit, for a hospital, for help. I followed not long after in what I helplessly think of as our parents' second miscarriage. We as a family didn't live there long. Only long enough for us to put our first couple years of grade school behind us. In that short time (and I am glad it was short but not for the reasons people might think) we saw and thus were able to learn what America was up to and, more importantly, what, if it had its way, it had in store for us. The country would be quite content if we stayed dead (you know, as well as I do, that most of the country thinks we are all gone). And if we were stubborn and insolent enough to remain alive it wanted us to live and die in some white woman's kitchen or to repair some white man's roof until our bodies gave out. It was there, in Washington, that I almost gave them their wish when I was struck by a car on my way to school. It was your first day as a crossing guard, and the car—running a red light—hit me at "your" corner. Of course, I don't remember much— just the mustard-coloured blur of the panelled wagon, the scream of tires. I don't remember that the car ripped off the top of my foot or that the mirror hit me in the face, and my skull, having bounced off the pavement at the corner of Connecticut and Nebraska, was fractured behind my right ear. But you remember this. Because you were there. As the rush hour traffic coursed around my body you jumped in the roadway and directed the cars around me to make sure I was not struck again as I lay, almost dead, on the pavement. You quite literally saved my life. Anyway, it wasn't long after the accident that we moved back to the rez. I found out, decades later, that our mother—barely thirty and by then a mother of four—said to our father: "I'm taking the kids back to Leech Lake. You can come or not." He came.

I hated it. You did not. But it's only now that I can see the gift that it was. She didn't agree with white people about who she was and what her life was supposed to be like. Nor did she agree with them about the shape of the world—that it was neatly divided between the civilized and the savage, good and bad, safe and unsafe, the nice and the ghetto, or the town and the rez. The gift of our return was not to be measured by the house we lived in, or the schools (all of them bad, all of them racist) we attended, or the food (stale, watery, wilted) available at the grocery store. Her decision to move back gave us nothing less than our Indian lives. We grew up knowing our family. And knowing our Elders. And knowing our traditions—ricing, hunting, fishing—that have kept our people alive through times much harder than either you or I can imagine. The gift was growing up as she did, where she did, and to some degree how she did: knowing who we are.

And how you've made such good use of that gift. It was that and not much else other than your energy and ambition that allowed you to defy this country and our fellow citizens who are quite in the habit of telling us who we can be, where we can go (and where we can't), and what we can do and what we can't. You cracked the Ivies and went to Princeton (where I followed you). And, at the end of your time there, you announced that you were moving back and were going to become fluent in Ojibwe and apprentice yourself to Archie Mosay (at the time, the most potent and longest-serving of our spiritual leaders). I was skeptical, to say the least, and—even though I should have known bet-ter—chalked it up to the kind of thing Indians say when we want to stun or impress white people. But you did it. You moved back home and devoted yourself to our ways. You sat with Archie. You sat with everyone. Most people see the privilege in those opportunities: you had access and opportunity and good fortune. What they couldn't see was the labour, the effort, the sacrifice. I could. I know how hard you worked. I remember how when we were living in Milwaukee, you drove across the state every weekend to sit with the old man, to go to whatever drum was meeting, to learn. Most people also think the time you spent with our Elders was restorative, sweet in a narrow sense. But they couldn't see how difficult many of our teachers were, how brutal they could be, the degree to which their own traumas and troubles turned some of them into what we can safely say are assholes. You didn't bristle, you didn't object, and you took that along with all the other work and became what you are now: a man in the world and a man for our people. In ways less direct but no less—and taking my own measure, I think it's safe to say "much more"—importantly, you saved all our lives, as you did on that street in Washington for me. Over and over again. I didn't say it enough when we were coming up, and I don't say it often enough now, so let me say it here: I am grateful and proud that you are my brother. In fact, much of the reason behind this letter is meant to make up for the many years when I was not a good brother to you. (That you haven't always been a good brother to me is not my subject. That's for you to dwell on or write about, or both, someday.)

I—having lost my innocence long before you, having become brittle if not bitter, and quite literally having left some part of my mind on the street back in Washington—have a cerebral knack for finding and saying the meanest thing. It really is a gift. And over the years I have—in large ways and small—gifted you with some of my meanest. I teased you about your shoes. I teased you about your choices. I teased you about your life. And it was profoundly unfriendly, not to mention unbrotherly. We all keep our lists and play our tapes of past harms. And you, having quite literally despaired at my words, have earned yours. But (and maybe this is the real heart of this letter) it's so easy to hear the louder thing and miss the pulse of something else. It's sometimes easier to see or at least imagine what's ahead than what lies behind. It's easier, ultimately, to tabulate the evil without rather than fear within. But if we can manage to do that—if you can manage to do the harder thing—I hope you see something different.

I hope you see that I was there. I was there when, in college, someone at some party dissed you and I swung on him and kept swinging until someone maced me with their beer. I was there to see your shoes. I was there when you took over after Archie passed away and I was there to take the heat of those who were displeased that you took over at all. I was there to move you back to the rez after your short years in Milwaukee were over. I was there—always and often—when your world fell apart. And I've been there to be radically undiplomatic when you were forced into a narrower course. (I'm not listing my virtues for you or anyone else. The spirits know that would be a short list and which-soever of them that actually exist are easy enough to see for anyone who cares to look.) Niizhodenh: I'm sharing all of this because—as we look ahead, together, toward the future with one eye and the people's needs with the other—I've been tending to the ground so you can look to the sky. And, as a reconciliation, an apology, and a look to the future, I want to say to you and out loud: we need more of that sky, and we need more people like you (untrammelled, versatile, rich in possibility, innocent) to do the looking.

I also want, in closing, to point out one happy thing: we're middle-aged now! Considering all of the ways life (and white people) have tried to prevent it, it's somewhat miraculous to have emerged where we are and how we are. We've talked about it so I know you know this: nothing scares or unsettles them more than healthy, happy, productive Indians. Considering it's the last thing they want, I couldn't be happier that we've managed to stand in the way of that desire. So let's, please, keep doing it.

Have a happy birthday, brother. (I'd wish our country a happy 250th but I wouldn't mean it.) I'll see you soon.

David
September 2024
Los Angeles, CA

Nitôtêmak, future ancestors, can you hear me? I am reaching through space and time to tell you what you already know. Sshh, let the world become quieter, listen. Can you feel my voice thrumming in your bones? Can you taste this love, sâkihitowin in your spirit, in your soulflame?

Now is not the time to give up. We've been here before and will be here again. Now, like always, but more so, is the time for love. Feel how nipiy loves all of you. Fill your mouth with it, with me. No, don't go there, focus. Hear it call to the water within you, feel that reply pulsing. Subsume yourself in the silkiness of nipiy's embrace and let it enfold you. It is goodness. It is everything. Let it penetrate you, caress you, love every part of you.

≫≫

Feel the sun's energy connect, charge, and flow through your cells, blood, and organs, especially that one, but no, don't let me distract you. Flush your body with charge, activating everything.

You give me your resistance, your joy, your honouring of your ancestors past and future—the celebration of everything we are. You fill me with energy and make change possible.

You, and all those who hold you up, hold you close, walk beside you—you know the way. From the buried rivers underground, from kimiwan falling softly from the sky to all that is held in our tears—tears both grieving for the world that could have been—that should be—and tears of joy springing from laughter so hard it tears our ribs open, breaking and rebuilding us with its power. Every drop carves the path forward, for you.

→→→

Take care of me, so that I can take care of you.

You need me to move, think, survive, and thrive. Through me, you flow between your ancestors past and future.

I need you.

First, to listen.

Sit down beside me, listen to my voices, all of them. Love me, as I love you. Then care for me, for all that is in me, iswaswillbe in you.

≫

Our destinies have always been and always will be the same. When we remember that we are all relatives, we are strong and the path is clear. We merge to bring goodness, healing to all our relations, our kin, ourselves. Cooling and calming all that is broken in every plane of existence. Tâpwê, there are mountains in our path. But one step, one drop at a time, we have the power to wear down all that stands in the way, flowing through it to miyo-pimâtisiwin. Together.

Kâwiya pakicîhk, do not give up, keep moving. Keep your molecular and spirit bonds strong and your intentions focused. I am here with you, I am you. We are all us. Do not let chaos distract you, keep focused on the world that should be, and make it our future.

With consultation on Cree language and worldview generously contributed by Dr. Keith Goulet.

I have written and rewritten this letter so many times over the last twelve years. I first began drafting it in the summer of 2010 when I sat down with your fragile paper journals in the comforting quiet of the Winnipeg Archives while I was staying in the city with a friend. Since then I've thought about you at many junctures, particularly as I navigated graduate school in northeast Scotland. When I was living over there I thought about you and my other settler ancestors from those islands. I never did make it over to Ireland, where you were born in the 1780s, and according to my dad, studied at Trinity College Dublin. However, being in Scotland and visiting the Orkneys gave me a sense of the distance, both physical and metaphysical, that you and many of my other european ancestors travelled by boat to come to the First Nations' territories you (and they) colonized in so-called Canada in the 1700s and 1800s.

After many stymied efforts to write to you in the last decade or so, what better time to sit down and finally write this letter than in the days close to *Samhain*, when the wheel is turning and they say the veils between the worlds are at their thinnest?

In early 2020, I became violently ill following a trip to New York City. I had travelled there by train, and a little while after that I came down with what I assumed was just a bad flu. However, it was not the flu—it was an illness that changed my life. And it forever cemented your nineteenth-century medical legacy in my consciousness.

But I need to back up a bit to explain why you were on my mind while I fevered, coughed, shivered, hallucinated, and prayed through my illness. Thirteen years ago, I met the eminent historical geographer Frank Tough while I was studying at the University of Alberta. Frank has spent his entire career studying the Hudson's Bay Company Archives meticulously, and he has established a groundbreaking database of Métis archival documents that houses the stories of myriad families across the Red River Homeland, including the family you connected to through your Métis wives Elizabeth Isabella Dennet and Jane Johnston. When Frank and I met back in 2009, he scrutinized me briefly and asked, "Your last name is Todd? Are you related to the nineteenth-century doctor William Todd?"

My face lit up.

"I am! I am one of his Métis descendants! My auntie has dedicated years to studying him and tracking down archival material of all our ancestors!"

A few days later Frank showed up to work with an article by the historian Arthur "Skip" Ray. It was an article about you and your remarkable achievements as a doctor working in present-day western Canada. The article details how you stopped a smallpox outbreak while you were posted as the Chief Trader at Fort Pelly in present-day Saskatchewan in 1837.

It was unusual to read about a european colonizer *stopping* a smallpox outbreak, given that infectious illnesses and diseases were tools of dispossession and loss throughout the last six hundred years of colonialism here in the Americas and globally. But Arthur Ray's study of you is unequivocal: in travelling to the UK to study the Hudson's Bay archives before they were repatriated to Canada, he stumbled into the illustrious details of your career and your penchant for stopping illnesses both difficult to diagnose and treat during the first half of the nineteenth century.

I resolved then and there to learn as much as I could about your professional career.

For these reasons, you came to mind a lot as I became violently ill at the start of the novel coronavirus pandemic in 2020.

That autumn of 1837, as the story goes, some First Nations' traders came to your fort and conveyed concern that they were turned away when they tried to enter Fort Union to the southeast, along the Missouri River in North Dakota. They shared with you that Fort Union was under quarantine due to sickness. Given your training in western medicine, the circumstances they described piqued your concern. Forts were not quarantined on a whim in these heady days of the fur trade. If there was serious enough reason to shut down Fort Union to trade, you had every reason to worry about whether the sickness visited upon this fort was heading your way.

You were not a trifling man when it came to diagnosing illness. I had the good fortune to visit with both Frank Tough and Arthur Ray in early 2010. I sat in rapt attention as Dr. Ray shared what he had researched about you. He explained to me the mystery that is your famous investigation of the "York Factory Complaint." In 1836 you were dispatched to York Factory to investigate, and hopefully cure, the miserable predicament that plagued the trading post with great regularity. Somehow, you managed to figure out what the affliction was. However, you came down with it as well, suffering so acutely that those at the post feared you might die. But you pulled through. And the affliction reportedly never came back.

I remember Arthur sitting back in his chair in the restaurant we were in as he relayed to me his bemusement: "But he never wrote down what the disease or the cure was!"

The cause, and cure, of the York Factory Complaint remains a mystery to this day. One you took with you to your grave.

I smile a little tonight as I recall this encounter with Arthur Ray and his admiration for your medical interventions that saved many lives. Back in 2010, when I read Ray's research on your medical feats, I assumed you had scrupulously applied your positivist scientific training to ferret out the York Factory mystery and its source. But in the ensuing decade I have come to wonder if you might have been a bit more of a magician or healer than you let on. Maybe you were more of a magician and healer than *you yourself* knew.

I struggle, admittedly, between admiration for your work as a doctor and frustration—and, at times, even shame—over your role as an employee of the Hudson's Bay Company in displacing and dispossessing Native peoples. Your work as a doctor is inspiring, and I hold you in immense esteem for the curiosity and competence of your medical career. Reading your journals from Fort Pelly in 1837 and 1838 humanizes you in a way that would otherwise be so easy to dismiss if I only viewed you through a one-dimensional lens. But I also understand the complexities of all the relations both you and I hold. We are messy humans living in a messy world. And it is far too easy, albeit seductive, to ride through a story or a history superficially. But I owe you more than that. I owe you the time and consideration to try to understand you as a man enmeshed in very rich and dynamic fields of relations, both personal and professional. You truly are a complex person. A Scots-Irish doctor who fought in the Napoleonic Wars in the Royal Navy, and later a trader and mercantile bourgeois figure in Canadian history. But you are also a man who married into very strong Métis families and honoured your obligations therein scrupulously.

To be honest, the parts of your life that resonate the strongest with me are the moments when you stood up to your employers and spoke plainly of doing the right thing. (Which, by some accounts, they didn't always appreciate.)

And that is what you did in 1837 when you applied the precautionary principle to the reports shared with you by Indigenous interlocutors who explained that they were turned back at Fort Union. Arthur Ray describes your actions as follows:

> Although parts of these stories were conflicting, Todd concluded that, if there was any disease at all, it was probably smallpox; *without waiting for confirmation of his suspicion, he launched an extensive program of inoculation with cowpox vaccine.* This was the first time that the Jennerian type of vaccine was used in the west. Besides administering the vaccine himself, he taught chiefs and medicine men the procedure, supplied them with vaccine, and told them to inoculate anyone they met who had not been treated. He also dispatched vaccine to other HBC posts to the north. *Todd's quick action saved the lives of countless numbers of Indians inhabiting the Swan River district and the woodlands north of the Saskatchewan River* and greatly enhanced his already considerable reputation among the Indians as a man who possessed powerful medicine. (emphasis mine)

The legacy of your cowpox vaccination campaign, and your swift and unequivocal decision to inoculate people in your district, even if it might have meant spending a great deal of the company's money in vain if it turned out that you were wrong about a wave of smallpox spreading from the US, was courageous. Nearly two hundred years before my generation faced down a virus that we are still struggling with as we are gaslit with messages from public health officials and politicians to "learn to live with [it]," you understood that it is better to over-prepare for a deadly virus than *actively, deliberately, and hubristically under-prepare and downplay its impact.* Even with your successful vaccination campaign, the 1837–38 smallpox outbreak in the Plains was devastating, and you yourself admitted you were not able to convince all Cree and Assiniboine leaders in the region to use this method. As a result, some communities were deeply impacted in ways that they still remember today.

I am sitting here on the Pacific coast tonight, not all that far from where you were posted at Fort Vancouver, Washington, nearly two hundred years ago. As I am writing this current letter to you, I realize that I was writing to you all along throughout my SARS-CoV-2 ordeal. Back in May 2020, I wrote:

> In those early days after my birthday in January, I enter my sickness with the expectation of it being like any other flu. That I will struggle, fever, and probably rage incomprehensibly for a few days before emerging anew. Six years ago, when I lived in northern Scotland, I came down with a flu that left me delirious. On the precipice of a different rebirth . . .
>
> I expect this flu to be like that. Quick, wild, disorienting. But it sets about its work inside my body with voracity. It hits me like a truck. In the early days, I keep trying to work out, lifting 20 lb dumbbells as sweat drips from my forehead. At one point while I labour through a reverse dumbbell row, I hear a voice screaming

silently at me from across another plane and it finally clicks: this is not like other flus. This is something else. You are in danger, Zoe. You must rest. Immediately.

Maybe we relive certain traumas from our lives and the lives of our ancestors to help us clear the energy from our paths. In early February, in my second week of being sicker than I have ever been in my adult life, my cough worsens. When I start to cough up blood one Saturday morning, I finally make my way to a clinic. The doctor is cheerful as she explains away my symptoms as a "flu with a three-week cough going around Ottawa" and offers me some cough syrup with codeine and tells me to stand in a hot shower.

It takes another four weeks, one "normal" chest X-ray, two more doctor's visits, and countless nights spent praying I will not die as I struggle to breathe, before anyone will give me antibiotics. By week six, they finally concede I probably have pneumonia. By this point, I am in constant, relentless fear of death. It hurts so much to be out of bed. I wait three hours in the clinic just to see a walk-in doctor. I text a friend from the waiting room and tell him I feel like I might die. He coaches me [to stay alive]. I finally see a doctor who spends more of the visit chiding me for not having a permanent family doctor than she does zeroing in on what is causing my symptoms. The doctor never uses the words pneumonia [or COVID]. It is the pharmacist who tells me, as I pick up my medicine, "Oh, we usually only prescribe this dose for pneumonia." I sit outside the pharmacy holding the paper bag filled with antibiotics. And it finally hits me that I am so much more sick than the doctors have been willing to admit for six weeks. I start to cry.

A week after I was finally given antibiotics, Canada finally conceded that SARS-CoV-2 was circulating broadly within the country. The country began measures to mitigate its spread.

Inside the little attic apartment I was living in in Ottawa at the time, I felt like a strange and unmoored kind of time traveller as I coached friends through the illness, easing them into the shock that the sudden and momentous global event had on our collective lives in early 2020.

It was around this time that friends and family started to put the pieces together. A friend asked me, "Do you think you . . . might . . . have COVID?"

Nearly three years later I know unequivocally that I had it. And the long, tortuous recovery I faced, which stretched out over almost two years, is consistent with the thousands upon thousands of stories of long COVID that people shared in the ensuing stages of the pandemic.

As the doctors I saw in early 2020 continuously refused to consider that perhaps the virus had already travelled into Ottawa from the proverbial modern-day Fort Union (not by riverboat as in your day, but by the myriad daily flights that land in Ottawa from major hubs around the globe), I thought about you a lot. And wondered at how a nineteenth-century fur trade doctor, equipped with only cowpox vaccine and integrity, could be better prepared to stare down a deadly virus in the winter of 1837–38 than the modern doctors who were dismissing me out of hand in the nation's capital in early 2020.

You have taught me that it is not the time we live in, but the relationships and principles we live *by*, that matters the most. And I am grateful for the lessons your medical legacy teaches me as I try to be a good relative in my own lifetime and in my own work. I think of your leadership as I stare down government failures to prevent the wiping out of whole species of fish, a result of the lack of precautionary principle politicians are using in their environmental governance, along the rivers that you and my Métis ancestors travelled in your lifetime.

And, as I type this out, I realize this is just the first of many letters to you. Because you loom so much bigger in my life than I have ever realized. And I hope that, over our correspondence, I can puzzle out the many complexities of your life and legacy, and the experiences your Métis children, grandchildren, and subsequent generations of my ancestors faced as Canada came into being as a nation-state, stretching across myriad Indigenous homelands.

The country that I call home today, and the country that I write myself through and against.

kinanaskomitin. Go raibh maith agat. Thank you. Maybe it was a little bit of your medical brilliance that kept me going in the depths of that terrifying illness. Surely, someone beyond this veil was looking out for me on those nights when I was certain I would not make it.

I am grateful.

How is it that simultaneously I want your help and want you to leave me alone? That I recognize I cannot do all the work of healing the land with our communities by myself but don't want you to do it either? That I can respect and praise your skills and knowledge but do not seek them, out of suspicion of your motivations and intentions?

I find myself so often, in the same moment, happy to build bridges of understanding between our cultures yet wanting to burn that same bridge. Proudly taking up the space you helped make for me but not wanting that space. Telling you it's okay to make mistakes navigating allyship but bracing for the inevitable impact of the mistakes you will make that I will indeed judge.

Your allyship makes my life this yoyo. A yoyo that brings me to the highest of highs and the lowest of lows. Over and over and over. I am a living, breathing, walking contradiction. But what else could I possibly be?

Your allyship does not mean we are on this journey of reconciliation together. It is not us together against the colonial world. You are the colonial world. We are on vastly different journeys. Yours, rather one-dimensional. Yours, you can choose to stop and start and stop again at times of your choosing. At your convenience. This is my multi-dimensional life twenty-four hours a day. Yours, one of learning the truth. Mine, living it. Yours, one of processing that truth. Mine, having to listen to your processing. Yours, acknowledging systemic harms. Mine, waiting for meaningful change.

You come to me, dear ally, with a map. Expecting me to guide you on a journey that is not mine on a map that is not mine either. Where do you begin? Where do you go? I do not know. All I do know is that our journeys are mostly on parallel tracks. Occasionally they may cross, and I will inevitably end up in your oncoming path.

Understand my weariness. I am tired. I carry the stories of my family and the expectations of my ancestors in a world that tells me it wants to include me but never quite does. I watch with wonder at a world seemingly embracing our knowledges at last, only to see the rising of a new form of extraction. All in the name of reconciliation. Under the guise of your allyship. Within only a few short years, I went from having scientists tell me that Indigenous knowledges weren't worthy of informing academic research to an inbox full of "opportunities" for collaboration. I don't quite know what happened, and I think I am supposed to characterize it as progress. I have been told to be grateful. I want to be grateful. But I wonder, dear allies, are you pressured into having such gratitude for your job by others too?

My journey is confusing. I am both embraced and harmed by you. Sometimes both of those by the same person. I have trained myself to assume you are well-meaning. Most of you are. Some aren't. How can I tell the difference? How quickly the wolves in sheep's clothing are revealed when I don't fulfill the unspoken obligations of the tokenism thrust upon me. You tell me I don't have to respond to or deal with the wolves. An offer of the protection of your allyship, but these remain empty words as you leave the wolves in positions of judgment of my accomplishments. You don't know how many there are. There are too many to name. I am too vulnerable to name them anyway. They are in every colonial structure I must interact with to ensure my success.

We are here for different reasons. I have been here all along to serve our communities. To do work that contributes to our rights. Our sovereignty. To try to heal our earth mother. To reclaim, reconnect, and revitalize what is ours. To push back on the erasure. For so long, this was work I did quietly with my friends. With little financial support. Without accolades. Suddenly this work has become the golden goose to colonial funding agencies and institutions. And as if by magic, out of the fog, you all appeared. You called yourselves allies. We went from having our few friends from across cultures helping us string together the best efforts we could muster with what little we had. Suddenly there was a crowd of you knocking at our doors. Some don't even bother to knock. Others run right over us, leaving us choking on a dust made up of our work repackaged and our knowledges stolen. We are left to see it splashed across publications that are gatekept by the lot of you without our own names attached. Knowledge integration revered according to a definition determined NOT by us.

I feel thrust into a role of community protector. A role that I know is not appropriate or even mine to take. Communities may choose which allies they seek help from, but in so many cases, communities are not seeking that help. This is where my mama bear bubbles up. I know the trauma attached to what has happened to our lands and waters. I know the stories of those who have lived the impacts of these same climate events you treat like research opportunities. I feel as though I exist in a video game where I stave off the constant onslaught of ego-driven research of settler scholars suffering from white saviourism. Too often flying in like caped crusaders, denigrating yet at the same time relying upon the knowledges of our Elders, and leaving when your professional mission is complete. It isn't all of you. But it's a lot of you. Even some who, reading this, think it isn't.

There are saviours who feel the need to don a cape on my behalf. To fight my colonial battles for me. To assert and determine that which is indeed colonial. To become experts in what is rightfully ours. To claim spaces that are not yours. Colonizing decolonization. These are the overtly declared allies working with a hyper-vigilance for their perceived colonial constructs and barriers with a personalized mission to tear them down. I must ask you, is it your role to be the decider of what requires dismantling? I will tell you the answer is a firm NO. So often your self-directed dismantling is in fact the erasure of my voice, such that I cannot even tell you that you are dismantling the wrong thing. Then I am left to deal with the consequences of this new form of colonization. Your service is not to me, it is only serving to create new tropes of us. It is a new type of dispossession. My battles are not yours. My battles are often the ones you brush off as not being battles at all. If you are looking for belonging or a cause, you are looking in the wrong place.

I look in the mirror and wonder who I am. I see this supposed trailblazer. Worn out and tired and just wanting the freedom to do the work I am called to do. Instead, I am shackled to this allyship that has left me unrecognizable, the work I feel called to do mostly untended. I used to be open and positive and hopeful. That woman is still in there somewhere, but this person looking back at me is not her. I never wanted to be this reflection. In fact, I saw this same transformation happen to the other Indigenous people I know trying to exist in this colonial space, and I judged them. I swore I would never become what appeared to me to be jaded, harsh, grumpy, and suspicious. I swore I would never carry an energy that would scare well-meaning allies away. Yet here I am. To those sisters and brothers and Elders I judged, I am sorry. I didn't understand. You were not any of those things. You were worn down by the heavy load that you carried for me. For us all. It is my turn now. Thank you. I love you.

Understand, dear allies, how incredibly difficult it is being thrust into reconciliation while many of our families are reconnecting and healing. We are figuring out our collective and individual journeys while navigating how we interact with you. All in real time. On full public display. The complexities of which feel as though they are served up as your entertainment. Or it seems that way from your commentary on that which is not for you to comment upon at all.

I wish I had clarity on what it is that I want you to do. But perhaps that is the point. I don't want you to do anything of your own volition. What

I want is for you to listen. To take in these words and the words of other Indigenous people and then step back. Our words are not meant to compel you into immediate action, as compelling as they may be. Our words are meant to assist in your preparation, such that you earn the opportunity to sit in waiting to engage with us from the sidelines. Learn our histories. Learn our worldviews. Learn our science. Learn that none of it is for you to possess. Your action is a commitment to your own preparatory ceremony. Meanwhile, continue to ready your OWN skills and expertise that you are willing to offer as help when sought. When sought. When. Sought. Wait for us to call you into our circles as we see that your skills and knowledges may be needed to complete the pictures of our choosing. Then you may put that preparatory work into action such that you will not harm us in the process. Such that we will work together in a good way.

Meanwhile, get to know us. As people. Not as a means to your end. Build relationships that do not rest upon your own agenda. As we get to know you, we will know your skills. As we get to know you, trust can build. Have compassion for the unspoken burdens I carry. Respect the work I must do and the boundaries I must place to protect myself. Lift our voices whenever possible. Make clear to others that our sharing is not a free pass to take what we share as their own. Again, it is through your preparatory ceremony that you earn the responsibility of working with me, so I am not run over or dispossessed of these spaces that are mine. When you are invited into our circles, understand that the work you may ordinarily do in other contexts now intersects with a different axiology, where it has more meaning and is never separate from our people.

You may have heard the saying "Nothing about us without us." This has become insufficient in this new world of extraction. Where the dispossession has become sneakier. Repeat this, dear allies: "Nothing about us that is not led by us." You are to come along with us, when invited. One day we will collaborate in a good way, when you are further along on your journey of prepared allyship. For now, we can get to know one another.

All my relations,
Jennifer Grenz

Remember, we are the land.

We are defenders of the lands and waters, and the places on, above, and below our vast territories—including the spaces we can neither see nor access. This is a special role given to us long ago, a responsibility that is both a gift and an obligation. Our warrior hearts are very special and so inextricably connected to the heartbeat of Mother Earth that they are, in effect, one and the same. We have come from the land and return to the land, like all the animals, fish, birds, insects, and plants that share this planet with us. The earth beneath our feet helps us feel rooted and gives us shelter; the water sustains us, and the plants heal us, just as they do for all living things. We are all connected, and like the love and protection of family, we are better together.

The health of L'nuk—the people—depends on the health of the surrounding ecosystems, in the same way that our warrior hearts are connected to all the other warrior hearts in our Nations. Our heartbeats are synced with the heartbeats of every other living thing in our territories, in a way that is uniquely ours—uniquely Mi'kmaq, Wolastoqey, Anishinaabe, Diné, and Hopi. The beat of the drum reminds us of this connection—a vibration that we can literally feel move through our bodies. This is an attachment that transcends time and is carried with us in this world and beyond. In this way, we are never truly alone. Our ancestors walk beside us in this journey until we become the ancestors of our future generations—a circle of life that never ends.

Since time immemorial, our sovereign Nations have governed the territories of Turtle Island. Our Nations have passed down our histories, languages, and cultures to countless generations through our diverse communication systems, our ceremonies and practices, and our stories. Whether shared orally, through acting, in our art, or in written form, these stories contain teachings that lay out the morals, values, and principles by which we must live as individuals, and within our families, Clans, houses, districts, and larger Nations. Through these teachings, we have come to understand that our connection to the lands is an integral part of our identities.

Remember, our story is powerful.

Our story reaches back to a time which is beyond memory. Since time immemorial, our Nations were strong, powerful, and honourable. We had complex governing systems, economies, and trading networks regulated by laws and legal systems passed down for millennia. These societies were supported by our expert knowledges in medicine, science, physics, biology, math, and astronomy, as well as philosophy, history, politics, and the arts. Our diverse knowledge systems were location-specific and based on lived realities and outcomes, benefits, and consequences. Even our laws, legal systems, and protective/defensive strategies were based on our experiences and adapted over countless generations to meet the needs of our collectives. Our Nations commanded respect as laws required us to protect óur peoples and our territories. We guarded our territories from threats, which sometimes resulted in conflict and sometimes resulted in treaties of peace and cooperation with other Nations. These experiences resulted in the constant expansion of our relations with other Nations, and even political confederacies that lasted generations.

There is no start date or end date to our Nationhood. Nothing about our cultures was frozen in time. We changed, adapted, invented, discarded, borrowed, and shared knowledges, laws, and practices like any of the other societies throughout the history of this planet. Change was a natural part of life, and so our customs, practices, traditions, ceremonies, and protocols were also adapted over time to meet our ever-changing needs and circumstances. These adaptations served to ensure the survival of our peoples into the future, while also keeping us connected to the wisdom of our ancestors. In this way, everything we do is both traditional and "modern" at the same time.

Although our Nations were diverse—with their own languages, cultures, practices, histories, and experiences—generally, each person had a special role. Some of us were handed down our role from family members or Elders, while still others had to find their special place through ceremony. This was as true for the women as it was for the men. Depending on their home Nation, not only were women life-givers, but many also acted as providers, warriors, negotiators, translators, and ambassadors to other Nations. In some Nations, women chose the leaders; in others, they advised the leaders; and in still others, they were the leaders. Each person was an important part of their family, Clan, house, district, or however they related to their collective. Our peoples were beautiful and our ways were beautiful. We were free, independent, and sovereign as both individuals and Nations.

Remember, we are sovereign.

All of this may sound utopic, and that's because it is utopic. It was a time of independence and freedom—but that does not mean it was a mythical place without struggle, hardship, suffering, or loss. Whether we suffered internal political discord, periods of floods and drought, scarcity of resources, or inter-tribal conflicts, our Nations had the strength and warrior spirit to face whatever challenges came their way— together. As each generation passed, we sung songs, drummed, danced, told stories of our heroes, and raised our children with hope and excitement about the future. The good times and the bad were shared collectively, and our children learned from watching, listening, and emulating. Experienced warriors and hunters would mentor the younger ones. Children would be raised by their moms, aunties, uncles, and grandparents. Home was about love, joy, and celebration of life as much as it was about survival, maintaining relations, and fulfilling our roles as guardians of the land. We were free to make our own mistakes and determine our own futures. We were sovereign.

The strength which lives in our warrior hearts and spirits has always come from the unity of our collectives and our independence as

Nations. We know how secure we feel when our large extended family rallies around us in times of need. At the same time, we all celebrate when children go through the rite of passage to become adults and more independent from their parents. We are independent but not disconnected. In the same way, we know what a powerful force we are when we stand together as a Nation against threats. The Mi'kmaw Nation continues to push back against violations of our sovereign, inherent rights as well as our modern-day Treaty Rights. We keep winning in the courts and on the ground. These nation-based battles require that families and communities come together to support the Nation. Although our local First Nations have a degree of local independence, they are not disconnected from the benefits and obligations of the Mi'kmaw Nation or our collective rights and responsibilities as Mi'kmaw peoples to the land—Mi'kma'ki.

In addition to formal alliances between Nations, as evidenced through inter-nation treaties, confederacies (like the Wabanaki Confederacy), and other agreements, there are also those informal alliances that were situation-specific and/or time-limited. We've seen it throughout history and even into modern times, where multiple Nations come together to stand in solidarity with one another against injustice: Red Paper, Wounded Knee, Constitution Express, Siege at Kanehsatake (Oka), Idle No More, NoDAPL, NoTMX, Wet'suwet'en Strong, 1492 Land Back Lane, and Mi'kma'ki Strong, to name a few. We are still here, standing on our lands and resisting Canada's genocidal laws, policies, and practices, as well as racism, violence, and exploitation by corporate extractive and energy industries and in some segments of society. We have never given up. We resist, and when we stand in solidarity, we make the world take notice. We must stay united in our families and Nations to protect our lands and our peoples. We are sovereign and only we can decide our futures.

Remember, genocide is not our fault.

Genocide is the most horrific crime that can be committed by a state against a group of people. To be guilty of genocide, a state must have the intention to destroy, in whole or in part, a specific group of people, like "Indians" (First Nations). According to the *United Nations Convention on the Prevention and Punishment of the Crime of Genocide* (1951), a state needs to have committed at least one of five acts of genocide: (1) killing members of the target group; (2) causing physical or mental harm to the group; (3) creating the conditions of life so as to bring about the group's destruction in whole or in part; (4) taking measures to prevent births in the group; and/or (5) transferring the children of the group to another group. The *National Inquiry into Missing and Murdered Indigenous Women and Girls* (2019) found Canada guilty of all five.

As Indigenous peoples, we have experienced one of the most devastating and longest-running genocides in the world's history. We have lost millions of our relatives through historic and ongoing acts of genocide. Through its laws, policies, and practices, together with its actions and omissions, Canada has failed to act to protect Indigenous peoples. This has resulted in extensive casualties at the hands of both colonial officials and modern-day state governments, institutions, and agencies. Yet, throughout history, we are the ones who have been portrayed as "savages" who need to be forcibly assimilated—the "Indian problem" that needs to be addressed by any means necessary and regardless of the outcome—even if it means our suffering or death. From starvation policies and widespread abuse, tortures, and deaths in Indian residential and day schools and Indian hospitals to forced sterilizations, the foster care crisis, over-incarceration, and the crisis of murdered and missing Indigenous women and girls, Canada's genocidal practices continue largely unabated. Although Canada has accepted the finding of genocide, it has failed to take responsibility to end it.

State law enforcement, military, and national security agencies (especially the RCMP) have labelled us as criminals, insurgents, and extremists, but it is they who commit unspeakable acts of brutality, sexual assaults, and killings of Indigenous peoples with near one hundred percent impunity. Ironically, these agencies have often blamed Indigenous peoples, especially women, for living so-called high-risk lifestyles, shifting the blame to us. We must remember that genocide is not our fault. The many ways that our people struggle to navigate the minefield of genocide, or numb the pain of multiple, overlapping, and ongoing traumas, is a testament to our will to survive and not any lack of character on our part. It's no longer just state institutions participating in the violence and exploitation of Indigenous peoples and our lands, but corporate actors like the extractive and energy industries and private actors like human traffickers and gangs. Sadly, these offenders also include individuals in positions of power, like some doctors, teachers, social workers, and even next-door neighbours, who take advantage of the fact that there is little risk of personal consequences for targeting Indigenous peoples. Racism, misogyny, exploitation, violence, and sexual violence against Indigenous peoples have all been normalized. The intergenerational impacts of historic and ongoing genocide are not our fault.

Remember, we are warriors.

Our Nations have survived the longest campaign of genocide in the world's history because of our warriors. It has taken a significant toll on our cultures, and our Nations have suffered mass casualties, but they have not defeated us. Some of us may still be the walking wounded, but every day our people get stronger. Every day we find ways to push back against genocide. We are the resistance, living, asserting, and defending our sovereignty every day. We are the resurgence, standing in defence of our peoples, our lands, and our futures. We are still here as Kanien:keha'ka, Wet'suwet'en, Secwépemc, and Oceti Sakowin. The hearts of our warriors still beat as strong as they did in our ancestors. Their love, sacrifice, and commitment to protecting us are the reasons we are still here today. We know that so long as there is one warrior on the ground, we will be okay. But genocide is relentless, and even the most dedicated warriors get tired. We must do everything we can to honour and support our warriors.

Every victory we have had is a seed planted for the future—the inspiration we need to protect our collective futures. Our mothers, fathers, grandparents, aunties, uncles, and cousins all have a role to play in our collective resistance to genocide, the resurgence of our peoples and governing systems, and the revitalization of our languages and cultures. We know now that the traditional knowledge systems and practices passed down to us from our ancestors have the power to save the lands, waters, and all living things on Mother Earth from further destruction. Warriors have fought hard to protect all of this. Whether it's grannies on the front lines stopping mining companies or our youth on the steps of legislatures calling attention to injustices—they have won many battles. We cannot forget to celebrate those successes, whether it's a temporary delay of pipeline construction or an outright end to a proposed mining project—they are all wins. Similarly, our marches, rallies, teach-ins, vigils, and public education campaigns have moved the marker on public education and inspire solidarity actions to support us. These too are victories. We are winning every single day. However, if we are to sustain these victories, we need to bring our people home— all those family members who have been forcibly disconnected from our Nations through colonial laws and policies.

I am still on my own journey and have much to learn. What I have learned has all been thanks to my ancestors, extended family, community, and my Nation. All this knowledge has been infused with the teachings of other First Nations whose own cultures and lived experiences have much to add to our collective knowledge and strategies on how to move forward. They too have ancestors who have lived, loved, and passed into the spirit world and know our collective pains and our joys. I have also benefitted from the wisdom and experience of our friends, allies, and supporters who have taken up the call for action on justice for Indigenous peoples. Our allies make mistakes and have much learning to do, but their commitment to hold themselves to account and to follow our lead is exactly what our settlers' relatives are supposed to do. They have the numbers, the power, the wealth, and the influence to be powerful allies in a war for justice and have been part of our wins over the years.

Remember, we are all learning.
Throughout my life, I have spent more time listening, observing, and thinking about the words and actions of my Elders than I have trying

to be the one leading the way. By sitting back, I have been able to learn from the wisest of Elders and leaders, whose words inform my own warrior path as an adult. My learning journey is a lifelong one, one which continues with the benefit of my family, who can help me better understand my mistakes and the ways in which our thinking changes over time, based on our experiences. We can and do change our opinions. In every experience, there is something new to learn, which can and does change our actions toward others. That is not hypocrisy, that is how we learn and grow as L'nuk—as the people.

Some of these lessons have changed the way I see the world, and I certainly do not claim to have all the answers. In fact, some of my views now may well be informed by the wisdom of other Elders and future life experiences. All I can do in this moment is share with you some of the lessons that are guiding my life right now:

Don't judge our people for the ways in which they have managed to survive their traumas. Addictions, anger, depression, withdrawal, and even violence are all manifestations of the traumas they have experienced. We may have to keep our distance from those who have harmed or would harm us, because our health, safety, and well-being are central to our ability to be warriors. We just have to remember that those affected people are still part of our Nations, and we fight for justice for them too. We need to accept our people where they are at, and not where we wish they were in this journey of decolonization. We should always be the soft place to fall for our people, even if it means we must do it at a distance for our own safety.

Never focus so strongly on the goal of unity at the expense of speaking out against injustices within our own Nations. We have all been colonized, and the process of decolonizing our thinking takes time, but that does not mean we can be silent in the face of destructive colonial thinking. Any one of our people who decides to take up the role of a leader must always answer to the people for their actions. That is not division. That is holding our leaders to account, as our ancestors have done for generations before us.

Our warriors have suffered significant traumas and are on their own journeys of self-reflection and making amends. If we demand that our warriors speak with one voice, speak like a professional communicator, or be free of mistakes, character flaws, and criminal records, then we won't have any warriors left to stand with us. Remember how many of them got those criminal records from a racist justice system still trying to remove us from our lands. They are our imperfect heroes, sacrificing their personal safety and freedom for our imperfect people. We need every warrior who is willing to stand up for us, flaws and all.

The battle must be on all fronts. We should never be divided on false choices. Our people can make a difference inside and outside governments and institutions. We can advocate for our rights both domestically and internationally. We can fight against unjust laws in the courts and on the ground. We can do private teach-ins in our First Nations and appear in mainstream media to help educate the public. We can teach about our Nations in universities as well as within our communities, to our children. The battle must be on all fronts, and we all have a role to play, whether we are on the frontlines or behind the scenes. Teaching our children to speak our languages, raising our children in love, taking care of our Elders who have all the knowledge, and reconnecting our people back to our Nations are acts of resistance, resurgence, and revitalization. These are the acts of warriors with big hearts.

And for the younger generation . . .

Don't waste your time on nameless trolls on social media. Trolls, haters, and racists covet your attention and are desperate for you to share their hate with your followers. They drain your time, energy, and focus from our righteous battle. Engagement with *user1234567* may attract even more haters, demanding even more of our time in the rabbit hole of comment battles. These trolls cannot survive, nor can they build a following, unless you give them your followers. They can't spread their hate unless you do the job for them by forwarding, reposting, or responding to their vitriol. Similarly, don't waste time on people who are truly committed to racism, misogyny, hate, and destruction. They only want your attention to trigger the social media algorithm for their own selfish pursuits. We must apportion our limited time and energy in order to be strategic about what methods will have the most impact on social change for our people.

Remember, we are still here and not going anywhere.

Brother,

The other day, during a recreational hockey game, a man turned around and said to me, "I thought you were a woman." I had a similar experience at an airport, but with a woman. They see my braid down my back and assume it couldn't belong to a man. A few years ago, a co-worker at a big magazine in Canada made a joke—or what he thought was a joke—and in it he referred to me as a woman. More recently, at a fancy dinner at a prestigious college in California, a fellow writer said, "If I were Indian, I'd always have the two braids," at the sight of my hair rolled into a bun.

I want to say that I've gotten used to it, that it doesn't bother me, but that wouldn't be the truth. It does. But my love for my long hair outweighs all of that.

I want to say that I'm in awe of you. You've only known long hair. You and your friends have known no other life. You said you wanted long hair because I had long hair. And it's beautiful. It's your spirit. It's a symbol of our strength, because to wear it this way means something. Because there was a time when our relatives couldn't have long hair. They were taken away from their families, taken far away from home, where they'd be forced to look and act a certain way that wasn't natural to them. This caused enormous pain for generations of families, and still does. You probably don't know this yet, but you will, and I'm sorry for that. But it's necessary. I didn't always have long hair. I did as a child, but I cut it when I became conscious of all the other short-haired boys around me, scared of what they might say. I went to school off-rez at a young age and that made my insecurities worse. Mom never pushed me to grow my hair long if I didn't want to. And so it stayed short for a long time. Until I left home for university.

Having long hair, braiding it, feeling proud of it, has helped me feel closer to home, closer to you. And because we've never lived in the same place, I think often about the things we have or don't have in common, and how different we'll be when you're older, old enough to understand this fully. I left home as a young man to pursue a dream, and it's sometimes lonely—I miss everyone back home constantly—but perhaps if you ever do the same your braid will be a reminder that you walk not alone, but with me, your family, and your ancestors. It's a gift we share.

You should know how proud I am of you and your hair. How beautiful it looks. How beautiful you are. But you should also know that there will come a time when someone or something tries to shame you for who you are. But they will be wrong. They'll always be wrong. I was in Winnipeg recently, watching Mom braid your hair for a special evening.

You sat there quietly, didn't say a word, didn't complain as she brushed the knots out. You looked as if you were just thinking. Wondering about the world.

She did mine next. It was raining outside, you could barely see the street, and we watched it come down in sheets. And then we walked into the storm together.

Sweetgrass

I know, I know, how funny that I'm writing to you again. You're dead and this letter isn't going anywhere other than this page. I would say something sentimental, like I still believe I can talk to you despite all this. But the truth is I don't know about all that. I just miss you, and I know that sometimes it's okay to have a feeling and do nothing about it. But I wanted to do something about this feeling, this missing, and I can't really do much about it at all, can I? So I thought I'd try this letter. See if that helps the missing, even a little.

It's summer right now. The part of summer when the dandelions go to seed and sometimes get swept up in the wind, hanging in the air like white stars. For people with allergies, I bet that's kind of a bummer, but I think it's the most beautiful time of the year.

You died about fourteen years ago now. I guess that means you've missed out on a lot. First off, Garrett and Amanda have kids now. You'd be a great-grandma, a câpan!! I have never had much interest in having kids.

I didn't think I'd ever be able to love them right. But I also didn't know I was capable of the kind of love I have for my niblings. I didn't know that being an aunty was going to change my life. It's nice to know that this kind of love was always living in me, just waiting to come out.

I finished my undergraduate degree and then my masters. Now I'm a writer and I had a book come out last year. I make kombucha, which is a kind of fermented, carbonated tea, and I like to do puzzles and bead. Aunty Lesley gave me your old craft bag for Christmas a few years back. It had some coloured thread and squares of fabric with cross-stitched flowers in it. I think you were making a quilt. I used some of your pink thread on an art project recently. Because I wanted you to be a part of it. I want to finish the cross-stitching you started and sew the quilt together. I keep telling myself you'd want me to finish it. Would you mind?

You have missed some other things, obviously. Deaths, for one. Your mom died after you, as did a lot of your brothers and sisters. Aunty Doreen is the last one left, I think. She helps me with my Cree sometimes, and she wants to write a book about her life. I'm going to help her with that. Papa Don died this past September too. I don't want to harp on about these losses though. I'd rather update you on the good stuff. The joy of it all.

I met an Elder from Fort Vermilion in Edmonton a couple of months ago. Her name is Mavis. We had a connection when we first met, even before I found out where she was from. When I told her I was born in Fort, she asked who my family was. When I said the Smiths, she cocked her head to the side and her eyebrows pulled together. "Eileen and Robert?" she asked. I hadn't heard yours or Papa's name come out of someone else's mouth in so long. This is all to say that Mavis remembers you. She remembers how much you and Papa liked to dance, which is something I remember too. She said Papa was quieter than you. It's funny. I don't remember what your voice sounds like anymore, but I remember your laugh as clear as day. It's nice to know you laughed so much that it's stuck in my memory like that.

I wonder if you'd even recognize me now. I have tattoos and a septum piercing and a girlfriend who I love. I'm finding it hard to be loved back, if I'm honest. I wonder if that makes me look different than the little kid you knew who looked for love everywhere, like a hungry dog looks for food. Or maybe I've been this person this whole time, and you'd see me for who I am.

Sometimes I think I see you, you know. One time was at Native Provincials—Cole and Cory were playing for Paddle Prairie this past year. A little kokum with short, permed hair walked by and I swore for a second it was you.

Mom looks more and more like you every day, so sometimes I see you in her too.

Wanna know something funny? One of my most vivid memories of you is at Peace River, at the farmhouse. It pops into my head whenever I see a trampoline. It was summer, maybe around this time of year. Me, Garrett, Amanda, and Stayce were jumping on the trampoline and making you be "it" for dodgeball. But since you were the only person who was "it," you'd have to walk all the way around to get the ball every time you threw it. It's kind of a boring memory, I know. But I think I like it because I didn't get many of those with you. Boring memories, I mean. We didn't have a whole lot of time to make them.

Anyway, the wind has picked up, so I'm going to go for a walk outside. In a week, or a blink, the dandelions will be gone, and I'll have to wait until next year to see the white stars again. It's nice to look forward to things like that. I hope you get to see beauty like that, wherever you are.

JON HICKEY   *To My Sons, James and Spencer*

I'm often amazed by the precarious, even miraculous circumstances
that led to you. Sometimes contemplating that precariousness gives me
vertigo, and at other times it's just a passing curiosity, a stray thought
easily batted away. The alternative pasts my mind conjures are just fiction; the reality is that you are here, and you are both happy and healthy
and the best people I know.

You were both born in the city of San Francisco. As you know, I was
born in Mankato, Minnesota, a small town in the southern part of the
state. From there, my mother and father and I moved to the north side
of Chicago, the same city where my grandparents, Sully and Zella,
moved during Relocation. It was there that your Anishinaabe ancestors
adopted the ideals of the post–World War II American Dream: a respect-
able trade (electrician, in your great-grandfather's case), a mortgage, a
new Ford every two years. They left their Anishinaabemowin language
and customs in Lac du Flambeau and didn't return for a long time.

We moved to Milwaukee when I was as old as you are now, Spencer. We lived on the shore; my first memories are of looking down our street, past the sand-coloured breakers, to see the silvery surface of Lake Michigan and whatever was beyond the horizon. Your water is the Pacific Ocean, and I assume your imagination takes it as far as mine did. After a few years in Wisconsin, we moved to Minnesota. Northfield, a college town, and then onto Apple Valley, a St. Paul suburb. I graduated high school there and went to college in Madison, grad school in Ithaca, New York, and finally, San Francisco. Which is where I met your mother.

Every step I've taken in my life, every new town, every new identity, has taken me a little farther away from what your ancestors called your real home: Waaswagoning, or as the voyageurs called it, Lac du Flambeau. It means Lake of the Torches, and it's what I see whenever I hear the name. It calls to mind a memory from when I was about the age the two of you are now, a half-memory, really, an image of being in the boats with my uncles and cousins in the dark of night as they fished for muskies with high-powered lamps and spears. Lake of the Torches.

I remember beautiful country and bracing poverty. My mother always told me that I belonged here, and I was proud of this place. And it was something that we never really thought about because it was always there. It always is there—your grandmother has just moved into the house that my aunt lived in before she died.

Your mother was born in San Francisco and has lived here her whole life, except for a few years in medical school. You have known no other home except for this city. You have also not known the semi-itinerate, just-above-the-poverty-line upbringing that I knew in my childhood, nor your mother's childhood, her parents, and the recent-immigrant hustle. As I write this, I'm proud to say that we are fortunate and want for nothing. We have achieved things our grandparents could only dream of. And one of my fears, along with whatever routine parental anxieties we have, is that you will take this for granted. That you will not build from this.

So what is your conception of that place, Lac du Flambeau, nestled up near the Upper Peninsula of Michigan, near Superior? We took you there for the first time last year. We met your relatives. We went out to my uncle's cabin on Big Crooked Lake, and James, you marvelled at the loon calls echoing around the bends of the lake. You brushed the lily pads and swatted at the mayflies. You danced a muskie lure over the side of my Uncle Ed's boat. You felt the wind carrying off the surface and, for a moment there, you forgot about your beloved MUNI trains and the noises of the city where your heart is.

But what about this place? Do you hear your name in the drum? Or in the sighs of the pine forests? And if you don't, what would it take for you to hear it?

Perhaps this is the source of my fear. Relocation, boarding schools, the Termination Act, all of those were a targeted policy of removal, one that looks successful in its purpose of killing a culture. There's a certain kind of shame, on my part, of not doing enough to fight against this loss. The fight is difficult to wage so far from home—there aren't very many Anishinaabes around here, and none from Lac du Flambeau. My opportunities to go back are limited because so much of my life is here now. I suppose this is common for travellers like I was in my youth.

I will tell you this: I associate the most spiritually resonant things in my life to the reservation and its people. It is the nexus of life and death that I know, the land of my imagination wherein lies the answers to my questions about what this life is about, and where it goes when it ends. We were never church people in any sense. Your mother had a Catholic education, and your grandmother occasionally goes to mass, but we never had any allegiances to any denomination, nor did we have any community. I've stepped into some churches and found nothing inside them that called to my soul. I wonder and worry about that side for you—I've never adequately answered it for myself.

Is it fair of me to ask of you to take on this burden? You are enrolled. You had the required quantum to be Anishinaabe on paper. You receive per capita payments. You will owe the tribe in ways that you don't quite realize yet. But your roots are here, in San Francisco. You were born in this city. Your grandmother is from Hong Kong, and your grandfather is from China. You have more Cantonese than Anishinaabemowin, and you honour their traditions more regularly. Which is how it should be. And how do you honour all of these things adequately? I don't know the answer and probably never will, because this is your life and your burden and your source of strength. This is your legacy.

In the end, I will love you for whatever you do with this. But I hope that eventually your heart does point its way home, to Lac du Flambeau.

Margaret, I don't know exactly where to start. You are one of my aunties and I wish we met and spent time together. I know that my grandfather had three wives. That was not uncommon or wrong; it was survival during the early 1900s. I don't know which of those wives would have been your mother, but I don't think it matters much. I don't think it matters at all. Blood is blood and family is family no matter what.

I know small bits and pieces about you. The way I know the bits and pieces of all my family. There's nothing written on paper anywhere, but we don't need paper. We aren't white. One of my brothers met you once in Winnipeg. He said you looked like a cross between both your sisters and not exactly like either of them. One of them was my mom and she was always very silent about you and everything that your lives contained. Harder times then, hardest times too.

I know that the three of you were taken away to residential school. I know that you were the one who did not comply. The one they locked away inside a mental institution because you were "untrainable," and you were released years later. The brother who visited you says it was a partial lobotomy that had you released. You lived out your days in Winnipeg. Had a tiny apartment. Went to and from the hospital where you worked in the laundry. You smoked cigarettes. A quiet life. A silent and singular life.

Canada is starting to wake up to it all. In 2021 unmarked graves started appearing—the children finally shaking a country out of its sleep. Canada is back to being reconciled. The Pope came along and offered his apology. I like him and I hope healing begins. What I hoped for more than anything is that you would have been alive and able to hear him, along with your sisters.

There are so very many stories that will never be made public. Never published. Never spoken. Never heard by anyone. But I want you to know, Margaret: I wrote about you. In the story I wrote, you were Margarite and you were the heroine. You were the one who saved your sisters and all of you ran away from the school. I made you strong and savvy. I made you outfox the colonial characters that tried to make you "trainable." I have never spoken about any of this publicly and now it is time. Time for others to know the brutality that we each work at recovering from. Time for them to know that your life was not for nothing.

Margaret, the auntie I never knew, know that you are loved and that you live on inside me. N. xo

CODY CAETANO

A Supposedly Impossible Shot
of Five Daughters in Tandem

MJ

If our lives amount to seedlings and fibre, the western sky transplanted yours before mine broke dirt and got weaved into a duster flung easterly. I suspect a forty-year holdup before you and I can release the bags from our shoulders and eyes and run into the other's hug, commencing an unexpected and wholesome visit. Official notice can't discern whether you called a lean-to shanty or an oleander grange home, so we'll settle for a compromised epistolary. Because I only know so many ways to heap niceties about you onto a page, and the varied minutiae I got approximates little beyond a moonlit collection and a rueful, blurry composite. Digging you up net the rest of us six lines, the likely-false belief that you lived wrinkle-free, and a centerpiece photograph from your wedding set to background the apps, clock, and the lock and home screens. Lo, I know that is more than most get, and below your interlake bouquet is a watch or corsage, can't tell which, although in it I can see that we both inherited these slim wrists. If the heat gets me for too long or I don't wake at four in the morning, you are right there, floating in tandem with the deep: wub-wubbing between slot-machining dreams and the breach of reality that a good sleep eases me into. Because you still take stock of the future, eyeing it up long after your shoots hewed a grove. Making it look so easy. And maybe it is.

MR

If our relations cleave a natural, sinewy grain, you chopped to keep us out of the weeds. On my best days, you get busy, shooting white cowboys in a black canyon or dancing on Creator's bar, wrangling the twang that binds a season to a day, and a runaway to a place. So much has changed since that brief, one-time-only week spent together, eh? Never mind how the trip animates you into breakspeed fruition, at least enough for me to get your sobriquet zapped to a pec, done less to express a sentimentalism than to celebrate your aesthetic range. We make sort-of visits, I think: like when a cardinal greets me on a birthday, and my dad says cardinals make pretty good angels on the call. How many flaps and gusts until Arizona? Is that you before me, necking around the deck railing? I'm figuring out if you are the desire to wake and acclimate to the day, the french press spurt that burns my chest and wrist, or the gauze and bandages that hug the oozing wound thereafter, taut yet soft, keeping the slugged bubble that grew wide and fat and off-yellow overnight until it popped, scarred, and eventually healed anew. You, the slimmest membrane in the universe. A partition.

AM

If our relationship to language courses the narrowest strait, yours charted a way. On my worst days, you email me poems. And they are good. The celebratory boom of a small but mighty drum group. Formally and ethically and spiritually, your diegesis reveals the afterimage of history without lapping it up. You write toward the heat and on your feet, washing dishes or when you're walking Buddy. Penning the investigation of a lifetime too, awaiting the quest and the dance and the moment to hang it all out again, because you know how good it feels to heal. And even with four days and nights of no water or food and the birthrights you did not know were yours, you came to love the earth. Of course. You remind me to do so every time we chat, even if you don't make such reminders explicit or say as much. It's all in the lilt and leap of your talk. And I'll never forget when, in the middle of the night after a long day of poker games and snowstorms, you walked over to the couch to wrap me in a blanket, and left me thinking for hours in the dark of our annual family Airbnb. A thick, everlong commitment to warmth and cozy.

KV

If our time here foments challenge and growth, you swooped in to prove it. I think it was you, before anyone else, who asked why some of us treat the nest as sacred and others not so much; how some irrigate the dry field and others irrigate the field to death, depending on how much earth they got in their pockets. You kept our hands out of ours, taught me to celebrate tomorrow, blasting our favourite songs when light seeped through and from the bays, spraying the Clorox that wrought dirt-free headaches, allowing the span of an evening together to liberate us from deficiency, and how inevitably those feelings carry a future-tense. Because of you, I learned that a good story keeps no secrets, and that the only difference between a good story and a bad one exists entirely within the teller, and whether said teller is able to embrace the bad and good all together. So even if the story of our time has plenty of bad, I like to think there is just as much good. Because where there is bad there is good. There just is.

TBD

If our spirits are meant to roam, yours will too. Telling you: in the pit of my eye and deep in my residuals, I feel you with me, by the water and above the dusky eve, agreeing to your life and getting ready for your descent. Sometimes I wonder if you're the last one in the chronos, and that with you, the webbed, intersecting gossamer will unglue from the branch to glide through the park, to join the innumerable stars dotting the cosmos beyond. Still too early to know because you aren't here yet. But when you come, remember what causes heart disease: living in cities (which can also cause stroke), noise inequity and lack of quiet hours, monoculture, blacking out at nuit blanche, unbalanced stress hormones that change the composition of blood and make our many vessels stiff, too much of anything and for too long, microplastics and worrying about them, and seed oils. More importantly, find ways to lighten the heart: weekending, healthy group chats, block parties, anything involving the number four (agreements, directions, medicines, and even -twenty if it helps), the opening notes to your favourite songs, and the truth that external forces can and will change the physical realm but got nothing on the spirit one.

you never talked about your secrets
the bad things you held
superstitiously close
as if giving voice
would only
let them out

lost your mom so young
moved to the city for school
didn't finish
married too young

baby boys all in a row
twin boys who died at birth
we don't even know their names
only that you refused
to return to the hospital
the following year
our next uncle was born at home

in the flood of 1950
when the river pushed too close
you left that house
never to go back
never to live so close

or trust
the water
again

you lost
husband
and son
the same year

how is this you?
these sad
empty facts
but

you're kneaded dough
made too quick and lumpy
you're burnt raisin pie
so good it's still talked about

you're the *Coronation Street* omnibus
every Sunday morning
all the characters you knew
better than your own cousins
and talked back to
yelled at
cried with

you are detailed lessons
on how to roll cigarettes just so
not too tight
but I always did
and you only smiled
smoothed the stuffed tube between your fingers
sprinkled out the extra tobacco
carefully piled
the medicine and swept
it back into the pouch
you are absolutely nothing ever wasted

you are Noxzema on a nightstand
stale scotch mints on the table by the door
in a fancy glass bowl
with the lid on
always

you are long
sleepy jokes
that made no real sense
but made you laugh too hard
before you even got to the punch line
you are full belly laughs
the kind that get into everything

even bad things
never let out

To My
                                              Great-Great-Grandchildren

Nwii-anishinaabem mii dash nisidotawiyeg.
I want to speak Anishinaabe so that you all understand me.

I hope that you don't understand these English words. I hope you need
help deciphering this letter. My dream is that you're growing up in a
world with Anishinaabemowin as your first language. I want most of
this message from your ancestor to be as foreign to you as a language
spoken on the other side of the world. I imagine you sitting with your
parents—descendants I likely won't see born in my lifetime—and they're
reading this to you slowly, then translating these sentences from their
memory of the English they learned growing up but don't use anymore.
I envision it being a strange but amusing experience for you all, but free
from the trauma and discomfort around our language that I and many
of your relatives struggle with as I write this note.

Geyaabi ninanda-gikendaan Anishinaabemowin.
I'm still learning Anishinaabemowin.

Maybe you'll have heard of me, your great-great-grandfather, and how I lived my life in the late twentieth and twenty-first centuries (if that's how you'll refer to this time I am living in). I became known for writing and speaking the English language. But I want that to be mostly insignificant to you and how you live in the future. Perhaps one day when you study English as a second language, you'll read my books and other writings and hear me speaking in old videos, if those all still exist by your time. Maybe all those stories and experiences will help you get to know me better, if you can understand what I'm writing and saying.

Minotaagwad gidinwewin iw.
That language of ours sounds nice.

If I had a time machine and we could speak face-to-face, I'd be able to tell you a little bit about myself in Anishinaabemowin. I could ask you some basic questions about yourselves, and then answer some of yours very simply. But soon, my speaking skills would be exhausted, and all I'd be able to do is listen closely to you, nodding at what I understand, and curling my brow at what I don't. But I would be able to follow most of what you would tell me, cherishing every word and second we have together. The thought of travelling into the future to hear you speak both delights and daunts me. But my dream of a future is a gift, something that was hard for even my father to imagine.

Aapji niminotaan Anishinaabemowin.
I really like to listen to Anishinaabemowin.

I hope you'll know that I have always been proud to be Anishinaabe. Same with your great-great-grandmother. I grew up in the homelands of our ancestors, on the beautiful island of Wasauksing in the body of water many of our people call Manidoo Gami, what others call Georgian Bay. But honestly, I've always felt a bit fraudulent of my Anishinaabe pride simply because I'm not a fluent speaker of our language. I very fortunately grew up in ceremony with a strong understanding of our culture and history because of our family's and community's hard work to revive and restore those ways in the aftermath of Canada's attempts at genocide. But the language wasn't embedded as strongly in me and many others of my age.

Nwii-minowe go.
I want to speak well.

Please be sure, I don't blame anyone in our family or community for my lack of Anishinaabemowin fluency. Your ancestors tried their best to pass down as much as they could to us, despite all the brutality they endured. I blame Canada for violently removing our language from them, which denied it to us in any fulsome and healthy way. I was still raised with our language all around me, and I feel lucky that it has been present throughout my life. But the intergenerational linguistic bond was damaged just enough to prevent its full transmission to me and many others my age in our community.

Dibaajimowinini indaaw.
I am a storyteller.

As I write this, in the year 2024, I'm doing my best to eventually become a fluent speaker of our language. I've returned to post-secondary studies at the age of forty-five to devote the majority of my time to learning Anishinaabemowin. My goal is to teach my three sons—your great-grandfathers and uncles—more than I learned at their age. If the work I've done up until now in English remains documented in some form, you'll know that I spent my professional life up until this point as a journalist and an author. Both careers have been remarkably fulfilling and rewarding. I've been able to travel the world and share stories with communities and cultures that I never imagined I'd ever reach thanks to my English language skills. It's been bigger than any dream I could have ever had as a little rez kid.

Eta nizhaaganaashiiwisidoon dibaajimowinan pane.
I always only write stories in English.

And while I'm proud of all that work and thankful for the opportunities my path has led me to, that's not what I want you to know me for. I hope you hear stories about how I tried hard to learn our language and was able to contribute to intergenerational reclamation and restoration of fluency in our family line. That's way more important than writing books and speaking to crowds in English. To me, my connection to that language is entirely utilitarian rather than emotional. I feel nothing strongly about English vocabulary, grammar, structure, and what have you. I enjoy using it to tell stories, and it's how I've made a living for a quarter century, but I'd trade it all to be a fluent speaker just for the sake of being able to raise fluent speakers.

Nwii-anishinaabemotawaag ngwisag.
I want to speak Anishinaabe to my sons.

That's not at all to diminish any other work Indigenous writers have accomplished to share stories in settler languages. They have revolutionized literature. This is just how I feel about myself. I have asked myself every single day since I began this language journey: How can I truly understand what it means to be Anishinaabe if I don't have intimate knowledge of our language? Can I truly call myself an Anishinaabe storyteller if I'm unable to tell a complete story in Anishinaabemowin? As I learn the nuances of how our ancestors and Elders spoke with one another, I am seeing the world in a different way. Our language animates and explains our existence and our universe in beautifully subtle and complicated ways that English simply cannot capture. But I don't need to explain any of this to you; you already know what a flower and a deer and a window have in common.

Nwii-nisidotawigoog.
I want them to understand me.

To cope with all my dismay, I have to regularly remind myself that it's not entirely my fault that I don't speak well, and as mentioned, it's none of our family's fault. That can't be said enough. This language—along with all the other Indigenous languages on what we call Turtle Island—wasn't supposed to exist anymore. If Canada had its way, our words and expressions would have been entirely erased. So the fact that I'm able to try to learn today is testament to the resilience and sacrifices of our ancestors who held onto these stories and speech despite the suffering they lived through. Even worse, many didn't survive colonial violence, and the knowledge and words that perished with them will never come back.

Daa-onizhishin.
That would be nice.

Nonetheless, I'm thankful for what we do have right now. Although the older generations are tragically dwindling, we still have some first-language speakers who learned Anishinaabemowin as children before their minds were tainted by English or French. The resources and initiatives to restore Anishinaabemowin are growing. And the collective will to teach and learn is stronger than it's ever been in my lifetime. But the clock is ticking, and that's why Anishinaabemowin will be my primary focus for the rest of my life. I'll still write in English to pay the bills, but my heart will be entirely in our language, motivated by my visions of you and your children never needing English or French as we do today.

Aambe anishinaabemdaa.
Let's speak Anishinaabe.

And perhaps in a few years, this particular letter will be obsolete. Maybe I'll have the skill and confidence to write you again entirely in Anishinaabemowin, and this will serve as a pithy diary entry only to document a moment in our family history. You'll have this one just to look back on my progress. And maybe you'll kindly laugh as I fretted through these paragraphs. But I know you'll understand this is all love, and even though I'll never meet you in this world, the love that's been passed down to you is ancient and has come through me, to which I've given everything I have. Speak proudly, live well, and take care of one another.

Gzaaginim.
I love you all.

Acknowledgments

This book would most especially not have been possible without our gentle, loving father, now Mooshum, who broke a cycle of violence and instilled in us the importance of advocacy. We would also like to thank Tara Walker, for planting the seed and seeing the need, Jared Bland, for creating space for this, and Kristin Cochrane, for your ongoing support and allyship. Special gratitude to the wonderful David Ross, for your insight, care, and vision. We are grateful to have you as our editor, and our friend. And to Kate Sinclair, for your beautiful design. Also to Marion Garner, Bonnie Maitland, Alanna McMullen, and Catherine Knowles on the Penguin team for shepherding this into the hands of our readers.

BILLY-RAY BELCOURT is a writer and academic from the Driftpile Cree Nation. He is an associate professor in the School of Creative Writing at the University of British Columbia. He is the author of five books: *This Wound is a World, NDN Coping Mechanisms: Notes from the Field, A History of My Brief Body, A Minor Chorus,* and *Coexistence.*

CINDY BLACKSTOCK, a member of the Gitxsan First Nation and Executive Director of the First Nations Child & Family Caring Society, was honoured to work with First Nations colleagues and children on a successful human rights challenge to Canada's inequitable provision of child and family services and failure to implement Jordan's Principle. This hard-fought litigation has resulted in hundreds of thousands of services being provided to First Nations children, youth, and families. Cindy was the recipient of the 2023 World's Children's Prize for the Rights of the Child, an award adjudicated by millions of children worldwide and referred to as "The Children's Nobel Prize."

CODY CAETANO's debut memoir, *Half-Bads in White Regalia,* came out through Penguin Canada's Hamish Hamilton imprint and was an instant national bestseller. It won the 2023 Indigenous Voices Award for Best Published Prose, made the shortlist for the 2023 Edna Staebler Award for Creative Non-Fiction, and made the longlist for the 2023 Toronto Book Award, the 2023 Stephen Leacock Memorial Medal for Humour, and Canada Reads 2023. It was named one of the best books of the year by *The Globe and Mail* and CBC Books. Excerpts of *Half-Bads in White Regalia* received the 2020 Indigenous Voices Award for Best Unpublished Prose. Cody is a literary agent with CookeMcDermid Literary Management.

WARREN CARIOU is a Red River Métis writer, photographer, and professor based in Winnipeg. He has published works of memoir, fiction, and poetry, and he has devoted much of his career to celebrating Indigenous oral storytelling.

DR. NORMA DUNNING is an Inuk writer as well as a scholar, researcher, professor, and grandmother. Her short story collection *Tainna: The Unseen Ones* won the 2021 Governor General's Award for literature, and her previous short story collection *Annie Muktuk and Other Stories* (University of Alberta Press, 2017) received the Danuta Gleed Literary Award, the Howard O'Hagan Award for short stories, and the Bronze Foreword INDIES Award for short stories. She lives in Edmonton, Alberta.

KYLE EDWARDS grew up on the Lake Manitoba First Nation and is a member of the Ebb and Flow First Nation. A graduate of Ryerson University (now the Toronto Metropolitan University), he has worked as a journalist for *Native News Online, ProPublica,* and *Maclean's,* and has held fellowships at Harvard and Stanford Universities. He has won two National Magazine Awards for his reporting and was named Emerging Indigenous Journalist by the Canadian Association of Journalists in 2019. He is currently a Provost Fellow at the University of Southern California.

JENNIFER GRENZ is an Nlaka'pamux woman of mixed ancestry currently living on the lands of the Pentlatch-speaking People. She is an ecologist working to help Indigenous communities heal their lands and revitalize their food systems.

JON HICKEY is a writer from Minnesota. He earned an MFA from Cornell University and was a Stegner Fellow in fiction at Stanford University. His short stories have appeared in numerous journals such as *Virginia Quarterly Review, Gulf Coast,* and the *Massachusetts Review,* among other places. He is a member of the Lac du Flambeau Band of Chippewa Indians (Anishinaabe). He lives in San Francisco with his wife and two sons.

JESSICA JOHNS is a queer nehiyaw aunty with English-Irish ancestry and a member of Sucker Creek First Nation. Her debut novel, *Bad Cree,* was shortlisted for the Amazon First Novel Award, and she lives in Edmonton with her brilliant girlfriend and their two cats, Alfredo and Olive.

WAB KINEW is an Anishinaabe author from the Ojibways of Onigaming First Nation. He lives in Winnipeg with his family.

TERESE MARIE MAILHOT is from Seabird Island Band. She's the *New York Times* bestselling author of *Heart Berries: A Memoir.* Her work has been featured in *Time Magazine, Elle, Men's Health, Orion, Indian Country Today, Guernica, The Guardian,* and *Best American Essays 2019.* She's the recipient of the Whiting Award and the Spalding Prize for the Promotion of Peace and Justice in Literature.

KENT MONKMAN is an interdisciplinary Cree visual artist. A member of Fisher River Cree Nation in Treaty 5 Territory (Manitoba, Canada), he lives and works in Dish With One Spoon Territory (Toronto, Ontario, Canada). His painting and installation works are held in the public collections of institutions such as the Metropolitan Museum of Art; Denver Art Museum; Hirshhorn Museum; National Gallery of Canada; Musée des beaux-arts de Montréal; Art Gallery of Ontario; and La maison rouge, Paris.

SIMON MOYA-SMITH is an Oglala Lakota writer and journalist. His work appears on NBC News, *Insider, Vice, Fodor's Travel, Lonely Planet,* and *New York Magazine.* Moya-Smith has a master of arts in Political Journalism from Columbia University and a bachelor of arts in Political Science with a minor in Ethnic Studies from the University of Colorado Denver. Along with writing, Moya-Smith teaches Indigenous Studies at the University of Colorado and is a frequent guest on Sirius XM as well as NPR to discuss Indigenous topics. His new book, *Your Spirit Animal Is a Jackass,* is forthcoming.

PAMELA PALMATER is a Mi'kmaw lawyer, professor, and award-winning podcaster from Eel River Bar First Nation. She is the owner of Warrior Life Studios dedicated to bringing Indigenous stories to life!

TAMARA PODEMSKI is an Anishnaabe/Ashkenazi multidisciplinary artist born and raised in Toronto, Canada. For the past thirty years, she has made a name for herself on stage and screen, and in the recording studio, amplifying underrepresented and marginalized voices. As an Indigenous storyteller, she is passionate about correcting the colonial narratives pervasive in the entertainment industry and is also dedicated to the integration of safe, supported practices within these spaces. Having grandparents who are both Holocaust survivors and Residential School Survivors, Tamara speaks openly about issues of intergenerational trauma, reconciliation, and inherited legacies of oppressed people.

Recently, Tamara launched Blackbird Productions Inc, a Film/TV production company committed to bringing stories to the screen in a trauma-informed way by using Indigenous Knowledge to guide the process from creation to completion. She believes it is possible "to tell our stories in a good way," without compromising the spirit, the heart, or the community.

WAUBGESHIG RICE grew up in Wasauksing First Nation on the shores of Georgian Bay, in the southeast of Robinson-Huron Treaty territory. He's a writer, listener, speaker, language learner, and a martial artist, holding a black belt in Brazilian jiu-jitsu. He is the author of the short story collection *Midnight Sweatlodge* and the novels *Legacy*, *Moon of the Crusted Snow*, and *Moon of the Turning Leaves*. He appreciates loud music and the four seasons. He lives in N'Swakamok—also known as Sudbury, Ontario—with his wife and three sons.

DAVID A. ROBERTSON is a two-time winner of the Governor General's Literary Award and has won the TD Canadian Children's Literature Award as well as the Writer's Union of Canada Freedom to Read Award. He has received several other accolades for his work as a writer for children and adults, podcaster, public speaker, and social advocate. He was honoured with a doctor of letters by the University of Manitoba for outstanding contributions in the arts and distinguished achievements in 2023. He is a member of Norway House Cree Nation and lives in Winnipeg.

NIIGAAN SINCLAIR is Anishinaabe from Peguis First Nation and a professor at the University of Manitoba, where he holds the Faculty of Arts Professorship in Indigenous Knowledge and Aesthetics in the Department of Indigenous Studies. Niigaan is a multiple nominee for Canadian columnist of the year (winning in 2018) and is a featured commentator on CBC's *Power & Politics* and APTN's *Truth and Politics* panel. Niigaan was recently named to the "Power List" by *Maclean's* magazine as one of the most influential individuals in Canada and is a former secondary school teacher who won the 2019 Peace Educator of the Year award from the Peace and Justice Studies Association based at Georgetown University in Washington, DC. He is an award-winning author, speaker, and curriculum developer, and was co-editor of *Manitowapow: Aboriginal Writings from the Land of Water* (Highwater Press)—the book voted by Manitobans in the "On the Same Page" competition as the top book to read in 2012.

MISS CHIEF EAGLE TESTICKLE is Kent Monkman's gender-fluid alter ego. Miss Chief often appears in his work as a time-travelling, shape-shifting, supernatural being who reverses the colonial gaze to challenge received notions of history and Indigenous peoples.

ZOE TODD (Red River Métis) was born in Edmonton and has spent their life imagining fishy worlds across the prairies. They are a writer, scholar, and artist working and living in Snaw-naw-as, Snuneymuxw, and Qualicum First Nations territories on Vancouver Island.

DAVID TREUER is an Ojibwe Indian from the Leech Lake Reservation in northern Minnesota. His book, the *New York Times* bestseller *The Heartbeat of Wounded Knee*, was a finalist for both the 2019 National Book Award and the 2020 Carnegie Medal. He is also the author of four novels and two other books of non-fiction, as well as essays and stories that have appeared in the *New York Times*, the *Los Angeles Times*, *The Washington Post*, *Harper's Magazine*, *Esquire*, and *Slate*, among others. Treuer divides his time between his home on the Leech Lake Reservation and Los Angeles, where he is a professor of English at the University of Southern California. He is also an editor at large at Pantheon Books, where his focus is on Native writers and emerging voices. Visit him at DavidTreuer.net.

RICHARD VAN CAMP is a recipient of the Order of the Northwest Territories and a proud Tłįchǫ Dene from Fort Smith, NWT. He is the author of thirty books in thirty years.

KATHERENA VERMETTE (she/her/hers) is a Michif writer from Treaty 1 territory, Winnipeg, Manitoba, Canada. In 2013, her first book, *North End Love Songs* (Muses' Company) won the Governor General's Literary Award for Poetry. Since then, her work has garnered awards and critical accolades across genres. She holds a master of fine arts from the University of British Columbia and an honourary doctor of letters from the University of Manitoba.

JESSE WENTE is Toronto born and raised and currently resides in Etobicoke with his family. An award-winning author and speaker, Jesse is a member of the Serpent River First Nation.

JOSHUA WHITEHEAD is an Oji-Cree/nehiyaw, Two-Spirit/Indigiqueer member of Peguis First Nation (Treaty 1). He is the author of the novel *Jonny Appleseed* (Arsenal Pulp Press), which was longlisted for the Scotiabank Giller Prize and shortlisted for a Governor General's Literary Award in Fiction, and the poetry collection *full-metal indigiqueer* (Talonbooks), which was shortlisted for the inaugural Indigenous Voices Award for Most Significant Work of Poetry in English and the Stephan G. Stephansson Award for Poetry.